THE DAUGHTERS OF GOD

KRISTINA S. FRANKLIN

To My Husband,

Jeff, you are my dream come true, I love you to the moon & back. May our love last forever and ever. Thank you for everything.

Edited by
TAKARA M. JAMES

Ever Thine
Ever Mine
Ever Ours
♡

Loving You 4 Ever

Kristina S. Franklin

9-14-20

WritLuxe

For information regarding special discounts for bulk purchases, please contact Writluxe Writing Firm at 615-240-7901.

Cover Illustrator - Twenty4 Studios

Interior Designer - Takara M. James

Typesetter – Takara M. James

Publisher
Writluxe Writing Firm, LLC
Takara M. James
5987 Lebanon Rd. Ste. 402
Murfreesboro, Tennessee 37130
https://writluxe.square.site/

E-BOOK ISBN: 978-1-7354496-2-3

PRINT ISBN: 978-1-7354496-3-0

Manufactured in the United States of America

CONTENTS

ACKNOWLEDGMENTS

To God
Without Him, this would not have been possible.

To my children, Justin, Kasey, Johnathan, Jason, Dorien, Jeffrey Jr., Jailyn, and Jordan. You guys are my air, my heart, my soul, and, most of all, my greatest gifts from God Himself. I love you all with eternal love. No matter what life brings you, always stay together as a family, follow your dreams, continue to help each other and please, keep God first in your lives forever. I'm proud of each of you. I love you.

To my mother, Karen Jackson Smith, you gave me the inspiration to write this book of journeys that were told by extraordinary women. Knowing that you have sacrificed a lot for my sister and I, made me the woman that I am today. I love you. No matter what anyone says, you raised my sister and I very well, and it has passed on to our kids and to their kids. Without you, none of us would be here.

To my sister Nina Taylor, you are my joy, my strength, and my best friend, thank you for supporting me in everything that I have ever done. Even when I broke things, fell out of trees, and almost electro-cuted myself, you were always there to cheer me on no matter what the outcome was. To my niece, Kenia (BEE BEE) Taylor, you will always be my sunshine. I love you. To Keith Taylor Sr. I love you, thank you for making my sister happy and thank you for your strength and braveness you give my family. Keith Taylor Jr., welcome to the family KJ, my loving nephew.

To my husband, Jeffrey D. Franklin Sr., thank you for believing in me when I beat myself down, thinking I couldn't be a writer. You pushed me spiritually towards my dreams and my love for writing. You showed me how to listen when God was trying to tell me something, to see what God wanted me to see, and taught me how to chase God when all I was doing was being comfortable with just knowing Him. You believed in me and never gave up on me, I love you God sent you directly to me, and I am very grateful.

To my granddaughters, Ja'Maya Renee, Olivia Marie, and Kaylee Denise. I pray that you three will read this and learn the rights and wrongs of being a strong woman. You will forever be my Fat Ma (Ja'-Maya), my Brownie (Olivia), and my Lee Flower (Kaylee). I love you, baby girls. Your Mimi did this for you.

To Mr. & Mrs. Daniel F. Jackson Sr. words cannot express how much I miss you and how much you are loved by me. You are the best grandparents on the face of this earth, and I will give anything to have you smile at me one more time.

Lastly, to all those who supported me, Thank You, may God pour out blessings over your lives: Twanta Baker, Justin & Stella Smith, Pastor Tommie L. Brown Jr. and the Christ In You Faith Temple Family, Torrik Townsend, Van Parker, Jalisa Anderson, Alecia Anderson, Tyronda Ward, Tyrone Smith, Derrico Jackson, Michael Tunstall Jr, Dominic Anderson, and Antonio Anderson.

INTRODUCTION

The stories you are about to read are based on events that have happened to some powerful women that I had the pleasure of meeting. Their stories are so unique and similar in many ways. Their individual stories are some of the most powerful testimonies I have ever heard, and I asked that they share it with others.

What God has done in these women's lives has given them the strength and courage to say, "Yes, I'll share my testimony to other women who could be going through the same things." Stories so clear that other's hearing it would know God will deliver you from anything if you let Him in.

These stories come from average everyday women, the lady who lives at the corner of your block, the one who comes to work smiling and cheerful all the time and seems to have it all. The hood girl who is too scared to give her life to God, and the woman who never has time to pray. The nice lady at the hair supply store who wears a lot of makeup and who always looks stunning, and the church lady who always makes the best peach cobbler.

These are women we see and speak to every day, but never stopped to ask how are you today? Do you need help or prayer for anything? Or just a simple, "May God bless you today, my sister."

One kind word can make a difference in a person's life, one act of kindness can change a person's mind. Hearing other women's testimonies can help you realize that you're not alone, and others have gone through the same situations. The question is, what if some stories don't have a happy ending, then what? That's when your testimony begins.

Here's the exciting part, six of these stories are true, and three are fiction, you choose what to believe.

Enjoy!

"The Daughters of God"

CHAPTER 1
EVA C. LASTING

My name is Eva Lasting, I'm a widower, a mother of two and a grandmother and great grandmother to the most amazing kids on the face of the earth. My story is all that I have in this hellacious world but, with God by my side through it all, I continue to carry on by faith and trusting in Him to be able to keep going. My story is a common one that I'm pretty sure a few women can relate too. By telling my story, I hope other women will feel comforted knowing that they are not alone. Overcoming pain is a period in my life that I am still battling to this day. Learning to be able to forgive is something that I still have not learned to do. Hopefully, by the end of this chapter, I can do that. I know for God to forgive my sins; I have to be willing to forgive those who have wronged me in the past. Some things just take longer to get over, and some things can leave scars on your heart that just won't heal. I feel that telling my story, I can come to a closer in my life, so when I leave this earth, I want to hear God say, "Well done, Eva, well done. My name is Eva Lasting, and this is my story.

My life has been a roller coaster, I've had good times, and I had bad times. But the loving part about it is that I'm still here. I'm almost in my 70's, and it will be a lot of things I don't remember, so my chapter might be smaller than the rest of the ladies you interviewed. It will be some things that I wish not to share because I refuse to live through that moment in my life again, but I will try. My story might be a good horror movie if this ever makes it to the big screen or a Hulu series. Can't do nothing but wish, and if it does, I want a back-row seat because you know folks don't like the front row anymore. I will skip my entire childhood because it was boring, but I will give you enough to go on, I guess. Don't get too comfortable Kris, this is going to be a short and straight to the point chapter for you. Probably the quickest interview of all times.

My childhood was simple, I traveled the world with my parents, and I saw a lot of things. I've been to France, Italy, Rome, Africa, Japan, Germany, Brazil and many other places, all before the age of 7. A lot for a kid, isn't it? Well back then, my family was a military family, and in the '50s and '60s, most women traveled with their husbands, family, and all. Life was good at that time; we were a well-off family who wasn't hurting for anything, and we moved around a lot. The only bad part about my childhood that I can think of right now is the constant moving, yes, I traveled the world and seen beautiful things, but, every time I got comfortable with our home and having awesome friends, we had to move again. That was the only downfall that I could remember. Hell, I was 7 years old, what could I possibly have an issue with? Not like the kids today, where 7-year old's have the right to an opinion. It wasn't like that back in my day, we had to obey our parents with no questions asked, and we could make a full course meal by the age of 10. Now, these young folks can google everything and won't feel the joy of getting out there and trying something new without a phone or a tablet in their hands, telling them what to do.

Get about 10 children together and ask them who knows how to sew clothes back together, how to fix something in the house that's broken without googling it, how to do grandmas home remedies for the common cold, or for sore muscles. I would say 2 out of 10 of those kids could probably do it. Ask those same kids who know how to go outside and be children without snap chatting your every move or posting your every thought and location on Facebook and seeing who has the most views on YouTube. None of them would be able too, everyone wants to be famous, and the world has made it where we can all be famous, damn shame.

I decided to skip all the high school stuff because I barely remember it anyway. High School was high school pretty much the same back then as it is now, no one really wants to go.

I don't think that's really going to change, those feelings are natural. I will say this, senior year will always, and forever be a kid's favorite year in school, that right there is just unavoidable.

I had a pretty decent up bring with my family, or so I thought. In high school, I was bullied because of my skin tone, I wasn't the color most people thought I was supposed to be. The ones who accepted me were the ones who treated me like a human being, and the ones that I felt I could relate to because of my parents were the ones who bullied me and almost made me kill myself. I slit my wrist when I was a teenager, and my family never told a soul except for my brother and my favorite cousin Mickey. Amazing. It's funny how families can hide so many secrets from each other and forget that God said everything covered will be revealed in the light, or something like that.

I'm going to skip all that other bull and go straight into what God has done for me and mine in the past years. I will go down memory so you can see how everything came together. But, sometimes, it will feel like God isn't there with you even through the bad times, especially when you married the devil, I'll get to that later, let's begin, shall we.

I met my first husband ------ in High school in Montana, our hometown then after graduation he was station in Louisiana and there, we had two wonderful girls. One was a charmer to many, and the other was a quiet little troublemaker that always got into stuff when she was a baby. That girl would crawl around and find the most difficult areas to get stuck in, even at 9 months old, that little girl was feisty. Their names are Emily and Phoenix. Those girls are my life and my soul, nothing on this earth will ever break our bond, not even death. I was married to their father for 4 years until I came home one day and caught him sleeping with the woman I had as my maid of honor at my wedding.

(Side note: friendship ain't shit when it comes to loyalty.)

Anyway, long story short, we got divorced, and my kids and I left. For a while, we stayed in a hotel until the money ran out, and then we started sleeping in my car because I know how my parents would react, plus, they would have made me go back to him. The Jacobson family had standards, that's how I was raised, we always had to keep up with the Jones, whoever the hell they were, I never met them.

To keep from going to my family's house to ask for help, I decided to get odd jobs around Louisiana to pay for a hotel, gas, and food until I build up the nerve to go back to Montana, where my parents where. I worked in New Orleans for about 2 years or so and saved enough money to move back home so I can get my own place and take care of my daughters.

After not dating for a while, I decided to get back out there and start dating again. I met this man named Charles Tucker, He was a funny person, grate personality, hardworking, living well, and not to mention a huge bank account. He stood about 5'8 and weighed maybe 195lbs dark complexion with a jerry curl and two gold teeth in his mouth. We dated for about six or seven months, and he adored my girls. After dating for that short amount of time, he asked to marry me, of course, I said yes, maybe this time I could have a real family. Marring Charles was not a good idea for my dad. Apparently, my father felt that I could do better, but they tolerated it because I had children, and I needed a family with a husband, yeah, right.

I was still in New Orleans, so we got married at the courthouse, and a week later, we moved to Atlanta. It's funny how things can go from wonderful to a natural disaster in just a matter of seconds.

Charles was the type of man that everyone wanted around them, the IT guy, the loyal friend who would go out of his way to help a person out. He would motivate people to do their very best in life. In the area, we stayed in, we had neighbors that would invite us to everything, BBQs, family picnics, and even to their children's christenings. Our favorite neighbors were the Parkers, and they were our best friends, Lilli and Vincent Parker. Lilli is from Korea, so we had many stories to talk about with each other. She worked at the nearby hospital as a registered nurse, and Vincent was a police officer that was built like the Hulk, maybe bigger. How he fit in that uniform was a mystery to me, but they were our friends.

One day we were at a Memorial Day neighborhood block party, and my girls were playing with Lilli's three girls, Becky, Bella, and Beth. Becky was 8 with long black hair that draped down her back with little ring curls, she was Emily's best friend. Bella was 7, her hair was sandy brown just like my daughter Phoenix, and those two were inseparable. Bella Died at the age of 15 because she had a rare disease she was born with. And then there was little Beth who was 4, she looked just like her daddy but with her mother's grey eyes and her father's mocha skin complexion. They were the cuties little girls you have ever seen.

Meanwhile, the men were having an ongoing debate on who could make the best BBQ sauce. Have you ever seen men in a pack of twenty, screaming and yelling about the right amount of butter and beer to put in a BBQ sauce? It was ridiculous, you would have thought they were talking about football or basketball or something. I saw our other neighbor Tom, Patsy's husband, stormed off and threw his apron down and screamed out, "It's the lemon juice man!!" and went home. We all started laughing and carried on with our afternoon.

Lilli and I were sitting in lawn chairs under a weeping willow tree for shade because the heat outside felt like an oven that turns all the way up to broil. For some reason, I found weeping willow trees very nurturing. I remember I had on this pretty white sundress that flowed down to my feet with pink and white orchids on it with the most beautiful colors or green for the leaves. My hair was up in a bun, and my shades were the color of my dress with a pink lens. Lilli had on light yellow capris with white flip flops, and her shirt had pictures of little yellow lemons all over it. Her hair was up in a bun too, and her shades were clear with a yellow lens. I guess you could say we were fancy for a block party in thousand-degree weather, but it was beautiful outside that we didn't mind the heat so much.

Lilli got up and walked over to the picnic table to get us some pink lemonade while we waited on the food to get ready. As she walked back towards me, I moved my feet out the way by crossing my legs, and that's when Lilli dropped both cups of lemonade. She stood there with a look of fear on her face, and I had no idea why. "Lilli, what is it?" I said in a frantic voice. She just stood there like a zombie, and I jumped up to look for our girls to make sure they were ok.

"Eva!" she whispered, "Come with me, NOW!" I jumped up and saw that the girls were ok, and Lilli grabbed my hand and pulled me to the side of the garage, so no one will see us. "Lilli, what is it? You're scaring me!" I said. Lilli put her index finger to her mouth and told me to be quiet or someone will hear us. "Lilli, what's wrong?" I said with concern. She turned to me and said, "Eva, I should be asking you what's wrong. I am your best friend, and you can tell me anything. Is there something you want to tell me?" she said with a look of concern on her face. "No, you know I would if something was wrong. Are you ok?" Lilli reached down and pulled my dress up to my calf muscle and said, "Explain that!" I was stunned, I forgot about the bruises. I was speechless, I didn't know what to say. How could I tell my best friend that my happy home was all a lie? So, I said the first thing that came to my mind. "Oh, that, Charles and I were putting up the girl's new bunk beds in their bedroom, and one of the bedrails fell and hit me on my legs. It's ok, no need to worry, I'm sorry that startled you." I said with a smile while I pulled the dress back down and shook the wrinkles out of it. "Lilli, let's go back to the party before our girls get worried because they don't see us. I'm fine, trust me." My heart was screaming help me, my hands were shaking, and I knew she didn't buy that story. Lilli turned to me with disbelief on her face and said, "Eva, I see you and your girls as part of the family, if anything is going on, you'll tell me, right?" She paused, Right!?" I glanced at her again while I walked away with a huge smile on my face and said, "Girl, come on here with your paranoid ass, I'm fine, it really was an accident. Quit trying to find stuff that isn't there, let's go, I have to get us some more pink lemonade now."

I continued to walk away, I turned and looked behind me to see if Lilli were coming and I saw her praying instead. I stopped for a minute and watched her with her head up to the sky, her eyes closed, and her hands reaching towards heaven. I should have run back to her then, but I didn't, I kept walking back to the weeping willow tree and sat down. We didn't say too much to each other under the tree after that.

Once the block party was over, all the women started to gather things to help the men clean up before it got too dark outside. I rounded up Emily and asked her where Phoenix was. Emily didn't say a word, just looked up at the weeping willow tree. There Phoenix was, sitting in the tree just looking down at everyone while they cleaned the streets up. "Girl, get down before you break your neck! I yelled. Phoenix jumped down with her dirty overalls on and her tennis shoes that were white this morning, now they are brown.

After we got home, I began to worry about Lilli seeing my bruises on my legs from my accident, but I shrugged it off. I put the girls in the tub and then off to bed they went. I walked into my bedroom to get ready for a bath myself when I heard the front door close. I stood in my closet to get my robe out for my bath, and Charles walked into the room. I didn't think anything of it, so I got ready for my bath. I pulled my summer dress over my head, and by the time I got it over my head, I saw a bright flash, and then I hit the floor. The first thing that came to my head was my girls, and I hope they sleep through this one. I pulled the dress off, and there he was standing over me. The look on his face was so demonic I had to shake my head to see if it was really him. Charles reached down and pulled me by my bun so hard that it came down then he drugged me to the bathroom and closed the door. I could remember thinking to myself that there is no God if He allows this to happen to his children. I was afraid for my life and my daughters' lives. Charles turn the shower on hot full blast and looked at me and said with demons in his eyes, "You thought I didn't see you run off with Lilli? B..!!!, I see everything! What did you tell her!?" he yelled. "What did you say to her, you little B...!!!?!"

When I looked up at him, all I saw was horns and a tail, or maybe that was the blood streaming down my face, and my left eye started to close. All I could remember that night was a hot shower with red water flowing down my back and belt marks on my legs. My girls were safe, and that's all that mattered to me.

I woke up the next morning with a headache and soreness all over my body. I heard the girls playing in the next room, so I knew they were ok. Charles never touched them, and I thank God for that every day. As I began to get out the bed, I realized that I couldn't move my right foot, like something was holding me. I pulled the floral comforter back and saw that this bastard had tied me to the bed rail, so I couldn't get up. I pulled and pulled, but I couldn't get it loose. I called Emily to the room so she could bring something to cut it and she couldn't hear me because the television was so loud. I laid in the bed for a minute to gather my thoughts, and that's when I glanced at the clock on the nightstand, and it said it was 4:00pm. I thought to myself, how long was I out this time. The last time I blacked out like this, Emily came into the room and told me not to worry about them eating because they already ate. Charles had fixed a big meal that day, and when he was done cooking, he fixed him a plate and threw the rest in the garbage, so my daughters could eat out the trash while I ate nothing. He made me watch Emily feed Phoenix out of the garbage can then said to me, with the eyes of Satan, "See, at least the girls are feed." Then the bastard laughed. Right then, I knew it was time to get out. I couldn't do this any longer."

Eva looked at me with tears in her eyes and said, "Do you know he beat me on our wedding night? He told me it was role-playing." I stopped writing and said to her with deep sympathy, "Mrs. Eva, I don't have to put this part in the book if you don't want me too." She lifted her head and said with a look of pain and embarrassment on her face, "No, because I just related to a woman who is going through the same thing, maybe one person can get the message from this, we can be blind by love and don't even know it. Keep writing, Kris." I wiped the tears from my eyes and said, "Yes, ma'am." I grabbed my pen and continued with her testimony. Eva sat up in her seat and began to speak.

"After about five months of getting beaten, I called my mother to tell her what has been happening, and she told me to stick with the marriage because no one wants to be alone. That's the price of a wife sometimes. Men get upset and do things they don't really mean. You had one failed marriage, so you need to make him happy and try and make it work. Can you believe that? My own damn mother told me to stay in this relationship with this man even though I told her that he beats me. I lost all respect for her that day. Also, she never told my father. Family, that's all I have to say about that.

I prayed and prayed many nights, nonstop for God to send us help, but no one ever came. Where was God now? He sure wasn't with my children and me because it kept happening. I couldn't leave because he always had the car, I couldn't run to Lilli house because she worked twelve-hour shifts and her husband did too. What was I to do but sit in my own self-pity and pray that he kills me so my children can go live with my parents?

One day, I was in the kitchen, and Charles saw me cooking ramen noodles for the kids. He kept all the other food locked in a cabinet while he was at work, so we couldn't get to it. He came in with a look of death on his face, and I knew this was the end. I knew he was going to kill me this time. He politely asked the girls to take their food outside on the back patio and play because he had to talk to mommy. I smiled at the girls and said, "It's ok babies, go ahead to the patio." I truly believe Emily knew what was about to happen because she didn't move. Phoenix grabbed Emily's hand and stood next to her sister, and she didn't move either. My girls were ready to defend their mother. I never saw them that united before. They both stared at him with I believe, murderous thoughts in their heads. They both had their hands balled up, and Emily had an old golf club in her hands that my father has given her on their last visit to Atlanta. Emily told me when my father gave it to her, all he said to her was, "Swing high and hard if need be." I didn't know about that until years later when Emily told me.

Charles looked at them and yelled, "I said go!" then he raised his hands at my children, and that's when I grabbed the first thing I saw and hit him across the head with it. I looked at my girls and said, "RUN BABIES!!!" Emily grabbed Phoenix, and they dropped their bowls and took off running out the back door. Emily never put down the golf club. My girls got away; I knew God heard my cries.

Charles got up off the floor and charged towards me, He grabbed me by my hair and pulled me to the bedroom. As I began to kick and scream, in the corner of my eye, I saw Phoenix jump the fence, and

Emily stood at the back door screaming, "Mommy!" with tears flowing down her face and her hitting the door trying to break the glass to get back in. That's when I knew I was about to die. I yelled back at Emily, "Good-bye babies, mommy loves you!" as he pulled me to the bedroom of death. Charles began to beat me in my face and head until I felt like I was about to lose consciousness. I felt him tie my hands to the bottom of the sink while he kicked me vigorously in my stomach. (That is the reason I can't have children anymore.) He grabbed a belt and started beating me with it all over my body and my face while he had the hot water running on full blast. By then, I had made my peace with dying and my plea to God, I just cried and waited for this to be over.

Charles took the belt and started whipping me in my face and arms until we heard a loud crash in the living room. Charles stopped hitting me and paused, then he ran to the living room, and that's when I heard him yell, "You B....!" I snapped out of my pain and thought, could that be Emily coming back in the house to help me? "Oh, My God!! He is going to kill my babies!" I didn't know where my strength comes from, but I tried to get out that bathroom, I couldn't untie myself quick enough. Then I heard a cry from the living room that still haunts me to this day. All I heard was, "MOM-MY!" real loud, and that's when I pulled on the rope so hard that I broke those pipes right out the wall. I got up and ran to get my children, and there it was, my prayers from God answered right before my eyes. It was Vincent, beating the living daylight out of Charles, I was stunned, my body couldn't move, I stopped breathing, and my heart filled with joy and I ran over to him and kicked Charles so hard in the face that blood flew on the ceiling. I looked over to the kitchen to get the butcher knife, and that's when Lilli came rushing at me with two other neighbors, and they got me out of the house. I couldn't see that well but what I did see was the other neighbor's husband rushing to the house and close the door slowly and started to walk towards Charles.

I could hear glass breaking, holes being punched in the walls, and for some reason, a belt is used. The sweetest sounds I have ever heard in my life was the first cries of my babies being born and the screams from the devil himself being tortured by the angels that God sent to protect us. As I walked out of the house, I looked around for my girls, and all I saw was Emily. I panicked because I didn't see Phoenix. I looked around and yelled her name, but she did not answer me, so I ran back to the house. Lilli ran after me with fear in her eyes and said, "Eva! Don't go in there!" I couldn't hear her; all I was thinking about was my girls. What if she's still in the house, what if she's trapped or ran away when I saw her jump the fence? Right then, Emily said in a low voice, "Momma, don't go in the house, stay here momma. Please." I stopped in my tracks once I heard the innocent, sweet voice. I looked at Emily, and I didn't see one tear in her eye nor fear on her face. I walked over to her and looked around the neighborhood and noticed no cops were called, no ambulance was coming and no sign of Phoenix. I grabbed Emily and held her so tight that she started coughing. "Emily, baby, where is your sister? Why won't they let me go in the house? Where is your sister!?"

Emily held me tight and took her eyes and looked up at the weeping willow tree in Lilli's yard, and there was Phoenix, in the tree looking at everything that was going on. Finally, Phoenix jumped down from the tree, and we all hugged each other so tight that we all lost our breath. Right then, my daughters and I made a pack with each other that no man walking on the face of this earth will ever put their hands on us, Ever! And if they do, make sure it's their last: no rules, no exceptions, and no mercy.

As I hugged my girls, I noticed that everything got quiet in the house. Lilli and the other two wives of the neighbors walked me to Lilli's house to clean my wounds and to feed the kids. Suddenly, I saw two men walk out of the house with towels in their hands with blood on them. One of the gentlemen looked at me and smiled, he came over to get his wife, and they walked home together. Vincent was the last one out of the house, not one mark on him. But still, I couldn't help but notice, the house was silent, no cops to come to arrest him or anything. What happened in that house? Frankly, I don't care what happened to that bastard, but I still wanted to know what went down in there, and I'm sure your readers do too.

Well, let me tell you what Lilli and Vincent said to me that same night. I kept looking out the window at Lilli's house because I just knew Charles was going to come snatch us right out of Lilli's home, so I kept getting paranoid. I glanced over and seen that Vincent was on the phone with Tom, the other neighbor that went into my house that evening. I overheard Vincent saying, "In seven days, we will go. But if we have to wait seven days." He held the phone for a minute, then I heard him say, "Goodnight, brother, see you tomorrow." and hung up.

Lilli grabbed the girls and took them to her daughter's rooms, where they were going to sleep until things calmed down. Lilli came out of the room with three glasses in her hand, and Vincent had a huge bottle of Crown Royal and a bottle of Jack Daniel's in his hands. We all sat on the couch, and Lilli grabbed some ice for my face. I looked at both of them and said, "Are you all going to tell me what happened? Do I need to file a police report or get my bail money ready?" Vincent laughed and said, "No, there is no need for all of that. We took care of it already." I sat there with a blank look on my face and said, "Thank you." no questions asked.

Lilli sat next to me on the couch and started to tell me what really happened. "Eva, remember at the block party when I pulled you to the side and asked you how you got those marks on your legs, and you told me you got them from putting the kids' beds together?" I lowered my head and said, "How could I forget? I thought you forgot about that." She looked at me and said, "No, I didn't forget. Well, while we were all cleaning up from the block party, Emily told me how you really got those marks. She begged me not to say anything, so I didn't.

But I did tell my husband. After that, we started watching the house and paying attention to the times Charles would leave the house, and when he came back. I ran outside one day to ask Charles were you home because you and I were supposed to go to the grocery store and he told me that you went to visit your parents in Montana. Or course, I didn't believe it because our daughters were secretly passing notes to each other through the gates in the backyard where they played.

This afternoon, Emily wrote a note to my daughter Bella that read, "Help us, the devil will be here soon. Please save my mother." Bella came into the house and gave the note to me, and I read it. My heart dropped, and my soul quivered just from reading it. That's when I called Vincent and told him to come straight home now. Vincent and Tom were already on patrol and was very close to the house, so he asked Tom to drop him off at the corner, so Charles wouldn't see the squad car pull up. He came into the house and asked me had I seen or heard from you today, and that's when I showed him the note. After reading it, he snuck out our back door to see if he could see or hear anything, but it was already too late. He heard you screaming and saw Phoenix jump the fence and heard Emily screaming mommy repeatedly. He hopped on his walkie talkie and told Tom it's happening, and then Vincent went around the front so he wouldn't let Emily see him because he knew by seeing him, Emily would call Vincent's name which would tip off Charles.

Vincent ran around the front of the house and threw himself into your living room window to get in because Charles had deadbolted all the doors in the house. That's when I called Carla and Patsy to meet me out front with the emergency kits because we knew what was about to happen. Vincent went into the house and beat Charles to the point Charles was screaming for mercy. That's when we grabbed Emily and Phoenix ran to the tree. Phoenix jumped the fence and told my girls that Emily didn't get out and that the devil was in the house. When I saw you through the broken window, I ran into your house to come to get you to safety. Tom finally showed up with John, Patsy's husband, and that's when you saw them go into the house.

Vincent, Tom, and John went into the house to show Charles how it feels to get beaten by real men. Every note that the girls sent to my girls were very detailed, all the way down to eating out of the garbage Eva. Please believe me when I tell you, no one blames you, and nobody is judging you from this situation. Everything that he bestowed upon you will get done to him, and I mean everything. That's why the men went into the house, and that's why no cops were called, yet." Within these seven days, Eva, we will nurse you back into shape, pray, and then we will get you the hell out of here. After that, you will never hear from him again. You are my friend, and as long as I am living, he will never touch you again."

Eva looked up for and minute and asked me could I stop writing for a moment while she collects herself. I went into the kitchen to grab some water for Eva and some Vodka for me because that story was unbelievable. About 15 minutes later, Eva said, "Let's Begin," I pulled out my pen, took a swig of vodka and began at write.

"I never set foot back in that house again. I later found out that Lilli had called my parents, and this time she only talked to my dad, and when he found out what was happening, he sent us three airplane tickets to Montana to escape the devils' den. Meanwhile, Vincent sat in his man cave chair and told me the reason why I shouldn't be afraid anymore. Vincent sat up and said, "Eva, we went into the house and fought him with all our might. We did not kill him because that would be murder. What we did do was tied him to the pipes in the second bathroom in the back of your house and gave him a good old fashion ass kicking. We punched him, kicked him, feed him the food out of the garbage can, and more. John beat him with the belt he used on you, and Tom kicked him in the face. We did this every day for seven days. We told him that he will be going to jail for assault on a police officer, domestic violence, resisting arrest, child endangerment, child abuse, and child neglect. All of this will happen in seven days. There is nothing to worry about."

Vincent sat back in his chair and started sipping his crown royal. I realized that God heard me the whole time. I knew God didn't tell those men to hurt Charles like they did, but I would accept it anyway. To this day, I never saw or heard from Charles again after the trial was over. This man told the judge that he was God; that's when the judge said, "Well, if your God, then I'm the rapture because I'm about to call you up to the sky, the Sky Lane Penitentiary up north in Chicago for 80 years. If I hear that you have tried to contact Ms. Jacobson (I had my name changed back to my maiden name) or anyone from the outside contact Ms. Jacobson, that would be an extra 20 years to life added. The court dismissed." When the judge pound that gavel, I felt a sense of relief, and a great burden lifted off me.

When I walked past Charles before they took him away, I looked him dead in his eyes and said, "I forgive you, I pray God to have mercy on your soul while you rot in hell." Do you know this man looked at me and said with an evil tone, "I am god?" Then he was escorted out.

Do you know how hard that was for me to say that to that man? I would rather cut out my own tongue and throw it into the pits of hell with him, that's how I felt at the moment. That goes to show you that looks can be deceiving, and love and lust are two different things. I knew I was married to the devil because every time he beat me, I swear I saw blood flowing from his eyes like tears, it really looked like actual blood.

The reason I told this story is that there are plenty of women out there that look like they have a happy marriage with the perfect family, but deep down inside, they are the ones hiding a big secret. It might not always be abuse as the cause, but it could be adultery, sexual abuse, drug addiction, money problems, disobedient children, gambling issues, and even battling with their sexuality. All of those can become secrets that they chose not to show the world because they don't want anyone judging them or worried about tarnishing their image. Some of us will just put up with a husband or a wife just because the money is good, and they are living well. I'm here to tell you that it's not worth it, at the end of the day, you will still be sad and depressed. No amount of money can heal what has already died inside of you.

God came and rescued my children and me from the hands of the devil. God showed me all the signs that Charles was a psychopath, and I chose to ignore them. He didn't show the signs of being abusive, but I saw how he was when he was angry at work or if he lost a card game with his friends. I just shook it off and thought that he was a man, now I look back, and I should have followed my first mind and said no to the marriage.

I was told by a friend of mine name Vance that our first mind was the Holy Spirit telling you what to do. Society says it's our conscience and our voice in our head that we hear when it says, "Don't go that way, don't say that to that person, watch out, or turn around and walk away." Then we yell out, "I should have followed my first mind." The Holy Spirit is that first mind voice in our head. Life is funny like that sometimes.

Three years have passed, and now I'm in my hometown, and I have started to rebuild my life back together. I became a truck driver around town, and my girls were in a good school. Life was good again. I was making my own money; the girls were well taken care of, and I was closer to family and good friends. Lilli and I talked from time to time as the years passed on, and we grew farther from each other. In 1989, I was told by Patsy that Vincent had died in the line of duty, and Lilli took the girls and moved back to Korea with her family. The pain was too much for her, and she had to move away. I hate that I couldn't be there for her like she was for me. She saved my life, and I will be forever grateful.

After driving trucks for about five years, I decided to become an auto mechanic as a side job. The guys on my shift taught me how to work on cars and even my own rig just in case it broke down on the side of the road. I took that knowledge and used it to help friends and family with their vehicles if they ever had hard times and didn't have the money for auto mechanics. That brought me so much joy to be able to lift others out of a difficult time. I never charged them, but some insisted that they paid me for the work, and I turned that blessing around and took that money and helped another person buy food for their family. I didn't take life for granted anymore, live the best way you can and do things for others, and God will always make sure you and yours are taken care of. I'm a living testimony, and I know God is real.

Later in life, my passion for helping others became stronger. I thought to myself, "What could I do to help others full time and still make a living for my family?" That's when I decided to go to college to become a registered nurse. It was a hard road to take, but with the support from my family and friends, I made it through. I dated a few guys, but I learned a valuable lesson from being with Charles, I never brought anyone around my girls, ever. I never got serious with a man, and if I felt it was going that direction, that's when I ended the relationship. That part of my life traumatized me, and I probably passed up a blessing of a good man from God, but I still pushed forward. I had a good relationship with my dad and my brother, so that was all I needed. They were there for me all the way up to them both dying, and I loved them dearly. Now my mother, on the other hand, was different. I loved my mother, and she loved me, but we were never as close as I was with my father and my brother. I always thought because I was adopted that she really didn't like me. Oh well, I'll never know.

My children's father was in and out of the girls' lives once we moved back to Montana, and he never helped me support them and never came around. As far as I know, he had married two more times and then left those women too. I think he has three more kids after that.

Screw him, I could care less, but for some reason, Phoenix is very fond of her father. I guess because she doesn't remember having to sleep in the car and in and out of hotels after he left because I was too ashamed to go to my parents. To this day, Phoenix loves her daddy, Emily, on the other hand, doesn't care one way or another. She was old enough to remember a lot of things.

As years went on, I met a man named Willie D. Lasting, he was a friend to a friend of mine, and we all hung out together. He worked for the city of Montana as a landscaper, and we all had BBQs at his house because he owns about 2 acres of land, and he would have pools and water slides, and trampolines for the neighborhood kids. He had no children of his own, and he took care of his mother. It's funny how things work together, and everything happens for a reason.

Willie and I had become good friends because he was an awesome person. With me being a registered nurse now, I helped him take care of his mother on weekends and after work three days a week. That went on for about a year, and we became more than friends, he became my best friend. One day he told me he appreciated me for the work I was doing with his mom and volunteering at his church on Sundays. That's when he asked to marry me. Of course, I hesitated for about 20 minutes and looked back over my life before I answered him. I've known him for about two years, and he didn't show any signs of being a deranged lunatic, and I saw how he was with the girls. So, I said yes. We got married in his backyard and only invited a few friends over along with his family. My girls were there, and my grandchildren. I was in my early 40's now, so what else could happen. We had a good marriage, I can honestly say, I was truly happy. Willie was the only husband I had that really cared about me and my girl's wellbeing.

God had finally let me be in a real happy marriage with a God-fearing husband that was on my side since I first met him. But all good things have to come to an end. After seven years of marriage, five grandkids, one daughter married, and his mother passing away, Willie took his trip to heaven due to heart failure and breathing difficulties. He died in 2003 at St. Francis Hospital."

Eva suddenly got up and went into the bathroom to gather her thoughts, that's when I saw the tears flowing rapidly down her face. I didn't stop her, nor did I interfere, sometimes we as women have to cry alone, we have to be alone with God in our prayer room. Not saying the bathroom was her prayer room, but if you really need to pray, we as women can make even the hall closet or the laundry room, our prayer room. Even standing in the kitchen while washing dishes can be our prayer room. We all must take time out daily to make room for Christ in our lives, He made room for us.

Eva came out of the restroom and sat back down in the chair next to me. I asked her if she wanted a cup of water, and she said with a smile, "No Darling, bring me a shot of that vodka you were drinking. If anything, that would get me through the rest of this story."

As I stated before, my story is going to be quick and to the point. As time went on, I decided to focus more on my grandkids and life itself. Now, I have seven grandchildren, three great-grandkids, two married daughters, and two of my grandkids are about to get married themselves. What else can a mother ask for? Both of my daughters are successful, Emily is a home health caretaker, and Phoenix works in a coroner's office. By this time, my father had already passed away, and we all took shifts taking care of my mother. She didn't have any serious medical illnesses, but just old age had kicked in. I love my mother; she was just set in her ways like elderly people, I guess. To make a long story short, my mother past three years after my father passed away from cancer, and it was just my brother and me to hold up the Jacobson name.

That part of my life is an entire book itself. Dealing with inheritance, land, estates, and more could drive a person mad, especially if you have no idea what's going on and constantly being lied to by family for years. All I can say about that is, you really can die and take it with you. It's funny how families can fall apart all because of money, and it shouldn't be like that. My family that I loved so much, never thought about me once they passed away. Now how do you think I feel after that? No inheritance, no land, no estate, not even a picture, was left to me. All these years and all these sleepless nights, I had of getting up and down with my parents and going to doctor appointments after doctor appointments were all for what? A thank you and goodbye? My brother got everything, he and his children inherited the Jacobson family fortune. Oh well, life is really disappointing at times, and you just have to roll with it. They should have left me in the place they adopted me from.

A year later, my brother died from a motor vehicle accident, and that just left me, the last Jacobson. I had to think to myself, was I even a Jacobson or just the foreign kid that they showed off to everyone. I started to doubt the love from my father and my brother that they say they had for me. Who really did ever love me? My girls, I most definitely know they do, my grandkids, my late husband Willie and Lilli, and Vincent. Now my brother's family has the whole estate, where do I fit in at? Why was I even a part of this family anyway? I found myself questioning God all over again. Yes, I was very upset because nothing was left to my children and me, all to Jonas, my brother's family. It hurt like hell, but I threw my hands up in the air and told God *thank you* anyway because I know he has a master plan for me and my real family lives. He has too, I been through so much heartache and pain all my damn life for it to end like this. It must be something greater he has in store for my real family, the family I birthed. But God is mysterious like that, I guess."

"Ms. Eva?" I said with the utmost respect. "What can women gain from your story? How do you think this powerful testimony would help others? and how is your relationship with God right now?"

I watched Eva Lasting gather her things together and sat up in the chair, sat tall with her head held high, her shoulders back, and she had a look on her face so powerful, so inspirational, that it made me feel proud to be a woman myself. I knew then that the spirit of God was on this woman.

"Darling, she said with a humble and dignified tone, "I am a child of God. I've been abandoned, I've been raped by my second husband, I've been beaten, almost starved to death, I've been hurt by my own family, I've been weak, I tried to take my own life, and I've been mistreated by so many people. After all of this, I'm still standing. I survived through it all. My children did not go through the pain I went through, and I thank God every day for that. He gave me strong women in my life to raise, and I call them Emily and Phoenix. God blessed me with a real marriage and a real loving family to keep me going. I have multiple trades and skills that I can do all by myself from driving 18 wheelers to fixing a broke down Chevy, and I went to college and became a nurse. You want to know what I would tell women right now? I would say to them, If God can bring me out of this, He will do the same for you. It will be times where you feel like God isn't there with you like the whole world turned a blind eye to your pain, and no one can help you. When my second husband was beating me, I remember thinking to myself, is this how Jesus felt when they beat Him before they hung Him on the cross. Every blow to the head, every whipping from that belt, every kick to the stomach I received couldn't come close to what Jesus Christ felt. But, by the grace of God, Charles couldn't kill me no matter how hard he tried, and no matter how close he came to it. I believe that a lot of women should read and study the book of Job in the bible. Once I drew closer to God, I knew that Job experience way more hurt than I did, and we both still survived. I can quote part of the first chapter by heart to you right now, please add this to your book so other women can stop and read the entire book of Job and then, and only then, will they see the power of God. Yes, Job is about a man, but don't we all go through what Job went through in his life at one point or another? I'll give you chapter 1 verses 6:12.

Job Chapter 1 6;12 NKJV,

(Now there was a day when the sons of God came to present themselves before the Lord, and Satan also came among them. 7 And the Lord said to Satan, "From where do you come?"

So Satan answered the Lord and said, "From going to and fro on the earth, and from walking back and forth on it."

8 Then the Lord said to Satan, "Have you considered My servant Job, that *there is* none like him on the earth, a blameless and upright man, one who fears God and shuns evil?"

9 So Satan answered the Lord and said, "Does Job fear God for nothing? 10 Have You not made a hedge around him, around his household, and around all that he has on every side? You have blessed the work of his hands, and his possessions have increased in the land. 11 But now, stretch out Your hand and touch all that he has, and he will surely curse You to Your face!"

12 And the Lord said to Satan, "Behold, all that he has *is* in your power; only do not lay a hand on his *person*."

So Satan went out from the presence of the Lord.)

You see, Satan Attacks Job's Character, Job Loses His Property and Children, and Satan Attacks Job's Health and Marriage (NKJV)

Chapter 2 verse 9;10 says;

Then his wife said to him, "Do you still hold fast to your integrity? Curse God and die!" 10 But he said to her, "You speak as one of the foolish women speaks. Shall we indeed accept good from God, and shall we not accept adversity?" In all this, Job did not sin with his lips.

After all Job went through, his own wife said *curse God and die*. How many times did we say curse God and die? Yes, it was times where I prayed for death when I gave up on God and even stop believing in Him. But God is so loving, he didn't let me go. He kept me, and He blessed me all the days of my life. The devil came for me, but he failed because God commanded him not to kill me. We all go through trying times, rather male or female, we all must believe in something far greater than this world, or we wouldn't survive. The devil will have his way with us no matter the circumstances. It's up to God and your faith in Him and what you believe in that would get you through. Everyone has blessings with your names on it, and God is holding it until you reach your hands and your heart out to Him to receive it. Despite what you are going through right now, at this very moment. It is still up to you how the story will end, you can end it with a victory through Christ Jesus, or you can be defeated by Satan. Even the things that are out of your control, no matter the outcome, because terrible things can happen to good people and bad people, God will be the One who keeps you and heals you. His timing is not our timing, and we all have to learn that. But, when God does show up, He always makes sure He shows out. He will have you praising in the middle of the DMV or the grocery store on aisle 9 while you trying to buy ramen noodles to feed your family.

Praise Him through your good times and praise Him through your bad, just like Job did, and look at how God rewarded his good and faithful servant. God fed the birds and clothed the fields, so why wouldn't He do that for you too, so why worry?

Matthew 6:26-29 New King James Version (NKJV)

[26] Look at the birds of the air, for they neither sow nor reap nor gather into barns; yet your heavenly Father feeds them. Are you not of more value than they? [27] Which of you by worrying can add one cubit to his stature?

[28] "So why do you worry about clothing? Consider the lilies of the

field, how they grow: they neither toil nor spin; [29] and yet I say to you that even Solomon in all his glory was not arrayed like one of these.

There is nothing on this planet that God cannot defeat. Forgive others who harmed you and did you wrong and praise Him at all times. Through death, through heartache, through abuse, through hunger, through eviction, through lights being cut off and your car repo, and even losing a job, praise Him, because something is coming in your life so big and grand that you wouldn't know how to contain it. That is how I made it, this moment right here, right now, is why I'm still standing.

I am a living, breathing testimony, my name is Eva C. Lasting, and the "C" is for Conquer, and this was my story.

May God bless those who read this and be filled with hope and strength for years to come. Amen.

CHAPTER 2
LILLY STEPPING

"Whoever came up with the phrase, (The grass is always greener on the other side) must have never been to the other side. I searched for the greener grass most of my life and still, to this day, never found it, all I saw was soil and weeds. Everyone knows that life is not that fairy tale that they tell little girls when we were younger, it's more like a fight for survival. You have to fight for a job, fight for your children, fight for respect, fight for your man, and fight just to eat.

All my life, there was something happening that was tragic, heart-breaking, devious, and downright unnatural. You see, I can't tell you how God brought me out of it because I don't believe in God, never have. I don't have a religion, and I'm not an atheist. Atheists have to believe that there is no God or no devil, right? So, to me, that's saying that you have to believe in them in order to not believe, so how can a person say that?

I agreed to be in this book just because I don't believe in your God, does not make me a hateful person, or what this one lady called me, hmm...? what was that she called me? Oh! Yes! She called me a sinner because I battled her on what she believed. By the time we ended that conversation, she yelled out, "May the Lord guide you and keep you, my sister. May He order your steps in His words." So, I looked at her and said, "Thanks, ma'am!" in my sarcastic tone. My, my... that was about a few years ago since that happened actually, I remember because that's when I had my car wreck and had to get airlifted to the hospital because I had broken my leg in two places when the car flipped over into oncoming traffic on highway 55 trying to go to New Orleans for the Essence Festival that year. The pilot said I should have been dead, but for some reason, all I had was a broken leg. Thank goodness for seat belts.

I was driving a pearl white 2013 Nissan Altima with snowflake seats, and my tags read, "Blitz" on them that I had gotten myself. I was doing great that year, everything was falling together, I had found that green grass all by myself and was loving the view, until the wreck. I believe we get what we attract all the time. I attracted a good life, and I got it, but only for a moment. I had a friend named Carmen Stafford, and she used to go on and on about how good God is to her and how He brought her out of the dark into light and how He can do the same for me. All I did was listen to her with very little comments because I respect everyone's belief methods, but that doesn't mean I have to believe. I gave her a nickname when we were little, and it stuck with her entire life. I called her "Karma." Karma used to get in more trouble than I did, but she always managed to get out of it. Eventually, it came back on here every once and a while.

Karma and I were best friends in middle school all the way up till......"

As I glanced at Lilly, I noticed that she was looking at her photo on the wall of two teenage girls dressing like Salt and Pepper, the rap group for Halloween with a banner in the back dated 1992. Lilly's hands began to shake, and her eyes started to water, so I got up and asked if I could get a glass of water. Lilly lowered her head and said in a real low voice, "Yea, sure you can, they are in the cooler on the floor." I walked over to the cooler and grabbed two waters and a paper towel just in case the bottle would be wet, but really to hand her to wipe her tears she thought I didn't see. I sat back down across from her and pulled out my pen and pad to continue writing again. After we took a drink of the water and I gathered my things when she spoke again.

"Krissy, have you ever had so much hurt and pain in your heart that you didn't have the will to live anymore? Like, have you ever had anger so deeply embedded in your soul that you literally feel heat rising from your skin?" she said. I put my water down and said with a serious look on my face and said, "Yes, Lilly, I have, multiple times during my 45 years on this earth. I felt it last night when I asked my husband to take out the garbage on his way out the door to go to work, and he took the garbage out of the garbage can in the kitchen and laid it by the kitchen door. I get up to go get a soda about an hour after he left, and that man left the trash by the kitchen door. I called him and asked him why he didn't take the garbage out, and he said, "I did, I took it out of the trash can and sat it by the door until you were ready for it to take it outside. You said take the trash out, you didn't say take it outside to the big garbage can. I thought you were getting the cans out the bathrooms too." Men.

"Lilly," I said with a smile on my face, "The rage I felt for that man last night was unhuman, God he must have known I was going to pop Frankie in the head as soon as he walked through that door that next morning. God protects husbands from wives when they do crazy stuff like that."

Lilly laughed and said, "That was actually funny. But I don't believe in God, so where does that leave me?"

I knew then, she was serious. Lilly took another sip of her water and began collecting herself.

"People hold on to so many things on the inside for so long to the point that they start to feel angry for no reason. They begin to become exactly like the people they feel made them that way. So how does God view people like me? Does He take his hands off you and let the so called devil have his way with you, or do He sit back and watch how much hell he can put you through until you can't do anything but pray to Him or pray to something? I always wondered did God and the devil bet on how far a person can be pushed until that person gives in and pray to one of them. Where is God when children get raped by family members, where is God when a person commits suicide, where is God when a woman has to turn tricks just to feed their kids or keep lights on in the winter? Where is He?!"

Lilly placed her hand on her head as if she had a headache, then slowly took a deep breath.

"Kris, when I was 17, I lived a life of partying, drinking, popping pills, and having sex with anyone that would give me attention. I'm glad I never got an STD or an unwanted pregnancy with a guy that wasn't going to be there. Growing up, I had a perfect life with my parents. I stayed in a big house in Watts, I had both of my parents in my life under the same roof, I got a Lexus for my 15th birthday and a Benz for my 16th birthday. I was top of my senior class at 18 years old, and I had great friends to support my goals, I thought. Most kids that age would have loved to live my life, but for me, I hated it. So many people viewed me as this rich girl who didn't want for nothing, they all thought I was stuck up, and the only friends I had were the ones I was given from my parent's friends because we all had to hang together because our parents were all friends.

I had a friend named Troy Landers growing up who was the nicest kindest guy I could ever know. He played baseball for Hillside High School, and with his many accomplishments, we all knew he was going to go far in life. Scouts came from all over the U.S. to see him play. They even paid coaches just to let them sit in on practices to see how he was when he was not on top of his game and playing around with the other teammates, you know, his downtime. Everyone loved him, teachers, principle, other students; even some of the police officers gave him special treatment just because he was that popular in high school. They used to call him, Troy "The Ball Breaker" only because when he played ball, he would hit the baseball so hard it would literally explode, it was the most amazing creepiest thing I had ever seen. People use to think we were a couple because we were always together, more like inseparable. His parents owned a restaurant that I will not name because it is very well known by many all over the world. Like me, we were very rich and very popular with everyone."

Lilly stopped in mid-sentence and had a look of joyous love all over her face. So, I asked her what she was thinking about that had her so lit up in the face. She turned to me with tears in her eyes and said, I loved him more than I loved my own life, Troy was there for me when I wanted to end my own life. He never asked me what was wrong or what had me so sad. All he did was look at me and held me in his arms until we both fell asleep. He would know something was wrong but never mumbled a word; he would come in my window at night while I was sleep and just wrap his arms around me and fall asleep next to me until the sun would come up. He was my love, my friend, my brother, and my angel.

One time he came over to my house to ask me did I know where we can go to have dinner that no one knew him or would recognize him. Folks treated us like celebrities when we were together, no privacy. So, I told him, yeah, let's go to a soul food restaurant named "Daniel's" on the southside of town. Before I could get it out, he snatched me up, and we hopped in his Dodge Charger, and we were gone. He was unusually happy that night, it kind of confused me because I didn't know if this was a happy laugh or a psychotic laugh. He worried me, but I didn't ask questions, I was just happy to get away from everyone.

While we were in the car, he was telling me how he felt about me and that I was his best friend and his first love. He joked about us getting married and moving to Paris, France where we can have a house in the hills with lots of farm animals, and Sheppard dogs named Chandler, Joey, and Ross, he liked the TV show Friends, and he wanted to name our daughters Rachel, Feebie, and Monica. Now that, I would actually agree with, I love Friends. Anyway, while we were driving, he was playing George Michael song "Father Figure" the whole time, it was actually on repeat, I thought he just didn't feel like changing the song so by the time we arrived on the Southside of Watts I had remembered that song word for word. I looked at Troy and asked him why he wanted to go on the southside, and all he said was, "I want to change up." I looked at him and said, "Oh, well, if you wanted change, all you had to do was stop playing that damn song and change the CD player." We both laughed, and then he said, that's why I love you."

We walked in the restaurant, and no one knew us, it was beautiful to not have people come to the table and talk about baseball or trying to sit with us. Not a soul there knew who we were, it was marvelous. We got seated at a table facing the window to watch the traffic go by and see all the so-called "average" people, that's what our families call the less fortunate. I hated my parents for that, all our friends hated their parents. So, while we waited on our food, Troy looked over to the next table and noticed a young lady sitting alone with tears in her eyes, he said, "Lilly, don't we know her?" I looked over, and I couldn't believe my eyes, it was Karma, she was sitting at a booth with just a glass of water in front of her and a towel with something red on it. I got up so fast, I almost turned the whole table over. I ran through all the tables and yelled out her name. The lady looked up and said, "Lilly!" with a huge smile on her face. She got up, and we ran to each other and gave each other the biggest hug a friend could give a person. "What are you doing here?!" I asked with a huge smile on my face. I grabbed her hand and pulled her to the table that Troy and I were sitting at, and we hugged some more. Troy noticed who she was, and he began to smile, and then he grabbed her and hugged her even harder. We all sat back down and gather ourselves. Troy looked over and asked the waitress if she could bring us another soda for Karma, and he ordered her the same thing we ordered.

"Lilly, I've missed you so much, I begged my parents not to move from Hillside, but of course they don't listen. How are you?" she said while fixing her clothes. I looked at her with a smile and said, "Same thing, different day." While we were talking, I noticed that Troy had stopped smiling, and he stared at Karma for at least five whole minutes. He grabbed her hand and said, "Who did this to you?" with concern on his face. I looked at Karma and Troy and said, "Did what to who?" then, that's when I actually paid attention to Karma's face. She had a gash over her eye that her hair covered up and a bruise on her collar bone. My mouth dropped, and anger grew within me. "Karma! What happened. And don't lie to me!" Troy got up and squeezed in the booth we were sitting in, so all three of us were sitting on the same side. He grabbed her and said, "Carmen, you don't have to tell us if you don't want too. I totally understand." I looked at Troy, and before I knew it, I snapped. I looked at him and said, "Troy! This right here, dude, is not one of those heartfelt ass moments you do with me, she's hurt! Someone did this to her! What the hell are you talking about! Back the hell up, dude, she going to tell us what happened!" Troy moved his hand and said, "I was just trying to tell her I understand, that's all." Karma reached over and held his hand and said, "Thanks, Troy, but I need to tell Lilly what happened. I want to tell her what happened. She is my sister, and I love her. God saved me from a rape that was about to happen, but I was able to getaway. The guy I was on a date with did this to me. It was our first-time meeting since we had been talking on and off for about four months now on this website called "Sasha's Secrets" it's a website for people who are married and want to hook up with people who are not married. It was a mistake; I never should have gotten involved. So, this is God's way of punishing me. I deserved everything I got tonight. Guess that's why you always called me Karma, Huh?"

Once she said that my heart was broken, and then I got filled up with so much rage that my eyes almost popped out my head. I looked at Karma and then glanced at Troy, and his tail was sitting there with a blank look on his face, looking like Bubba from Mama's Family. "What in the entire Holy Hell are you talking about? This bastard hit you, and then tried to rape you! If God allows that to happen, then you'll need to switch up on your beliefs, this is not karma from you dating a married man, this is attempted rape and abuse! What God do you serve?!! You have lost your damn mind! This man needs his butt put in two places, the ground or hell, but if I find him, he will experience hell before I put him in the ground, and I mean that from the bottom of my heart!" I was so angry to the point that I saw red, my body got hot, my soul was boiling, and I think I saw the devil gawking at me from across the room. I wanted revenge on the bastard that did that to Carmen. That day, I decided to stop calling her Karma. It's amazing when you call somebody something for so long that that person starts to believe that it is really what their life represents. People need to think about that before they begin giving someone a nickname.

After a while of us sitting there and talking, the food came out, and it started to feel like old times before Carmen's family moved away. We laughed and talked until about twelve that night. We drove Carmen back home, and we headed back to our side of town. Troy was quite in the car for a minute; then he turned on the radio to break the awkward silence that was in the car. I looked over and asked him, "What was the reason for us going to a new restaurant?" He looked at me and said, I knew you were going to say let's go to the Southside of town because you always talk about going over there." Then he turned the radio down and told me something that I thought I would never hear come out of his mouth.

Lilly took another sip of her water then excused herself for about fifteen minutes. As I sat on the couch wondering what she was about to tell me, she came out of the backroom and handed me a piece of newspaper that was about twenty years old. It read,

"Famous Baseball Player Troy 'The Ball Breaker' Landers was found murdered last night in Southside Watts outside of childhood friend, "Carmen Stafford" house trying to break up a fight between Ms. Stafford and her alleged boyfriend. Witnesses say the alleged boyfriend, Marcus Belgium, came over to the victim's house and began kicking and pulling at Ms. Stafford's door because there was another man in her home taking her things out in boxes and loading them into a van. That's when Marcus Belgium began to argue with Troy Landers, and a fight broke out between the two men. Mr. Landers went to his car and pulled out a baseball bat and hit the suspect in the head, killing him. When Ms. Stafford came outside after calling the police, two men jumped out of a Black 1967 Ford Mustang Fastback and shot Troy Landers four times in the back of the head and shot Carmen Stafford in the chest, killing both victims.

The two suspects never identified, drove off heading north on Wayward Street in the Mustang. Witnesses say, when Carmen Stafford got shot, she was able to get up, holding her chest and witnesses said she yelled out, "My name is Karma, what you have done to us, will come back on you in the Mighty name of Jesus!" then she walked over to her friend Troy and kneeled down next to him and said, "May God receive us with open arms." Then she fell next to him, and they both died just as the ambulance arrived. Another witness who wants to remain nameless said, "When I heard her yell out, her name was Karma, and it will come back on you in the Mighty Name of Jesus! The two men that were in that Mustang turned the corner and hit a fire hydrant, and the car flipped over and rolled into the gas station on the corner and blew up. Whatever relationship she must have had with God must have been a good one because those guys were unrecognizable when the fire department put the fire out."

After I read the newspaper clipping, I looked over at Lilly, and she had a blank look on her face, she was in a daze. I put the newspaper clipping on the table next to Lilly, praying that she would say something. I had so many questions to ask her off the record, so many things were unanswered. Were Troy and Carmen together? Were they a couple, and that's what Troy wanted to tell Lilly in the car? How did Carmen know they would be at that restaurant that night? Why was he moving her things out of her home into a van, and was the guy that fought with Troy Carmen's boyfriend? Did Carmen really live up to her nickname, "Karma?" Did Lilly have anything to do with any of this? I had so many questions, now my head was spinning with thoughts and curiosity.

Lilly sat up in the chair and wiped her face and took another drink of water. My heart was going out to her because those were her two best friends that died at the same time on the same day together. How did she handle all of this?

As I sat there not wanting to say anything, Lilly finally spoke.

"Well, Krissy, I guess you have millions of questions about that article? Let me explain everything that happened, and maybe you will understand why I am the way that I am.

Troy and I had a different kind of relationship, we were close for a reason, and he loved the fact that people knew we were a couple. It was like that through High School and college. We were the perfect couple, and nothing could take that from us. When Carmen's family moved out of the gated community we lived in, that tore my world in half. That's why he crawled through my window that night and held me until the sun came up. I was devastated that my best friend since birth was ripped right out from under me, all I had was Troy now.

I had other friends, but those two were true soldiers, real good friends. Everyone says they have many friends or no friends, but they all can agree that they have that one true friend that would go to hell and back with them, ride or die, and that's who Troy, Carmen, and I were to each other. Just so happened they rode this one without me.

That night when he wanted to go somewhere to eat and the reason why he was so happy was that he told me that he was gay. This whole time we had been friends through high school and college, he was gay. He told me that he enjoyed us being together because we look like a happy couple, which we were in so many ways. We did everything just like a couple except have sex because he honored the sanctity of no sex before marriage. He let people believe we were a couple because he didn't want anyone to know he was gay until he was ready for us to know, and I respect that now. The reason he was so happy that night was because he had just told his parents, they were upset about it because it goes against God's law, but they accepted it, and they accepted him.

He was so happy; I wish I could see that smile again.

When we reached the restaurant that night, he knew Carmen was going to be there but didn't think she was going to in the condition she was in. It was supposed to have been a surprise for me to get us all reunited again, I guess that didn't go as planned. Anyway, as time went on, we started hanging out again, and we told Carmen about Troy's sexuality, and we all just grew even closer together. Well, two months after we met Carmen in Daniel's Restaurant, Troy had just got drafted to a very well-known Baseball Team, and we all were about to move to another state with him so we could all be together. He had bought us houses on the same street right next to each other, so we can be neighbors just like we were in high school. What celebrity do you know that has done that before? Nobody! That day he went to Carmen's house to help her load the moving van, he sent me to the airport to buy our plane tickets to Paris, France to celebrate my 25th birthday that was the next day. While he was helping her load the van, the guy Marcus pulled up and thought that Troy was her new boyfriend and assumed that Troy was moving in with

Carmen. Marcus was the married man that had beat Carmen that night we saw her in the restaurant. She had broken it off with him because she realized that dating that married man was wrong in God's eyes, and Marcus didn't like that one bit, and that's why he attacked her that night. Marcus had walked up to Troy and asked him what he was doing and Troy being the type of person he was, he didn't say anything to him, he kept moving Carmen's things and ignored him and just let him talk. That's when Marcus punched Troy in the face, and they began to fight until Troy pulled out his bat that his father had just bought him as a gift for being drafted into his new team. It's funny because the bat was specially engraved by his father, and it read, "Knock 'em Dead Head Busser," and that's exactly what Troy did with one blow to the head. After Carmen called the police that night, she also called Marcus's wife and told her to come to get her husband because he was stalking her on her job and at home. Sorry to say, but when his wife pulled up, she witnessed Troy knock her husband in the head and killed him. She stood there for a minute and got back in her car and left. Some say she was even smiling when she pulled off. After everything that happened that night, both of my dearest friends were pronounced dead on the scene on June 14th at 12:00 a.m., Carmen's and I 25th birthday."

As I sat there on Lilly's couch in total shock and heartbroken, she got up and walked to her kitchen island and fixed both of us a glass of Hennessey Black and Coke with a cherry in it. This time, I can say, I needed this, then it hit me, today is June 14th, 2018.

"Kris?" she said in a low voice. Let me explain to you why I do not believe in God, why would things like this happen to good people like me? Why would God rip my soul right out of me on my 25th birthday and take my two best friends with it? Why in the hell would I believe in a God who hurts people for fun? Why am I still here?! Why didn't he take me with them? We came into this world together, and we were supposed to leave this world together! How could Carmen believe so much in this God that He allowed this to happen? No one can answer that question for me. Ever since they died, I have gone to almost every religion there is to get that question answered, and no one, I mean no one, can give me a suitable answer! Now, why you think that is? Because they all have doubt too, just like they say God said have faith as small as a mustard seed, well, they have doubted the size of a mustard seed as well. They just don't admit it. How much hell does a person have to go through to see this so-called glory of God? He's never done anything for me but caused me pain and hurt. Why would I believe in a God like that?"

As I watched Lilly stand there in her kitchen, I noticed behind her that my previous book I wrote called, "Searching for God when your Blind in Faith" was sitting on her countertop and I knew then that she is looking for Him but don't realize that He was with her the whole time. I put my glass down and walked over to her. As I glanced at her tear-filled eyes and her shaking hands, I told her, "Lilly, God was with you the whole time, you just didn't see Him because you were focused on the negative. A lot of people, including myself, struggled with belief. God was with you when your car flipped over, and all you had was a broken leg when you were supposed to be dead, He sent Troy to you that night to comfort you when Carmen moved away, He was with you when you were at the airport buying plane tickets to go to Paris for your birthday and not in the car with Troy that night they died. God is with you right now, giving you the strength to tell other women your story. God wanted you to tell your story, Lilly, to show your strength and His Glory. You could have been dead in that car or at Carmen's house, Lilly. But he wanted you alive because He knew I was coming. He is using you to help more women than you could possibly imagine, and now your story is going to be said to millions of women who are struggling the same way you are. He is here in this room with us right now, and I pray to God that your story reaches at least one who is contemplating suicide, a woman who doesn't have the strength to leave her abusive husband, a woman who is struggling with drugs or prostitution. God can use the weakest person to show His glory. God is not the author of confusion, nor is He an evil being. He is the Father of all things and guess what, He wanted Troy and Carmen right by His side to watch over you as you battle the devil in your time of hurt. He has Angles around you that are so strong and powerful that nothing on this earth or in hell can touch you. Walk-in your pain, walk in your doubt, walk in your worries, walk in your power, and walk-in your faith Lilly, but what you need to do is no matter what life throws at you to knock you off your trail and search for God, you need to continue to "Walk" my sister! Walk for Troy, walk for Carmen, walk for the women out there that are about to make the biggest mistake of their lives. With your story, you will be walking across the world, just like Jesus did preaching the gospel of His Father. Let the Holy Spirit use you to get closer to God and don't let nothing in this hellish world stop your stride, you are my sister in Christ and a Daughter of God! and I am here to walk with you Lilly, I will be there to help you get to the mysteries of your search, and I will be by your side until the good Lord calls us home to be with Him. You are A DAUGHTER OF GOD, OWN IT! You need to be at those pearly gates so you can hear those words that say, "Well done my good and faithful servant!" Those are the only words you need to worry about hearing once you leave this earth! You need to be with Troy and Carmen in heaven because that's the only time you will see them again."

Lilly dropped her glass and fell to the floor in tears and began praying to God on the spot. With tears in her eyes, she prayed to the Lord like she never prayed before, I got down on the floor with her, and we prayed together. She screamed out forgiveness for the doubt, for not being with her friends the day they died, and she yelled out, "Devil you cannot have my soul, I am a daughter of God, and I belong to Him, get out of my mind, stay away from my family, and get out of my house!"

We stayed on the floor for about 20 minutes just praying and yelling out to God the Father until she started repeating the word Amen repeatedly, thanking Him for everything that He has ever done for her and her family. I went and got her a cool towel and a bottle of water to calm her down, but as I noticed that God was working with her, I just stood back and continued to pray over her while she was in the midst of the Lord.

Amen.

CHAPTER 3
STORM CHASIN

"I always thought my name meant that my family was trying to be unique or name me something that flowed with chasing. It wasn't until the death of my uncle who died in a tragic accident on his job that my father finally told me how I got my name. On my 32nd birthday, which so happens to be the day of my Uncle Josh's funeral, my dad felt that everything he ever loved was taken from him.

My mother and father already had my name picked out after they found out I was floating in her belly, he told me my name was supposed to have been Isabella Marie Chasin, after my grandmother, my father's mother. The day my mother went into labor with me, she had just gotten over a bad case of the flu. One afternoon, she started feeling labor pains but thought it was just Braxton hicks, so she began doing labor exercises and breathing routines because she was only 36 weeks pregnant with me, and her due date was 4 weeks away.

That night, my uncle, who is my father's brother (Uncle Josh), came over to watch the football game with my dad. While he was there, he noticed that my mom was in pain, so he called my dad to tell him that he thinks Faith was in labor and that he should get home immediately. My dad was stuck in traffic on the expressway due to a bad wreck, so he decided to drive on the median to get off the expressway faster. My dad told him to call the ambulance and call my mom's best friend Stacey, who lived next door because she was the emergency contact and her labor coach.

It had begun to rain heavily outside, and the winds were about 37 miles an hour, so I was told. While my father tried to fight his way through traffic and the weather to get to my mom, he got into an accident himself, nothing bad, just a minor fender bender. He explained to the other driver in the wreck that his wife is in labor and he was trying to get to her, the other driver told him don't worry about it, and no harm was done and let him leave without exchanging information. My Uncle Josh and Auntie Stacey were with my mom once my father arrived with panic written all over his face. I was his first child, and he didn't want to miss anything.

My dad is one of the most amazing men I have ever known. His name is Theos Chasin, Theos in Greek means, "God." So, my father's name was God Chasin, my grandmother taught Greek philosophy in college, so I guess you can say she really enjoyed her job.

When my father arrived, he saw the ambulance outside and immediately jumped out of his truck and ran straight towards the house to be with my mother. Once he got inside, the rain had gotten so bad, that the paramedics said it was unsafe to drive and that she was going to have to deliver inside the home. My uncle used to tell me that it was so much blood all over the floor that it grossed him out, so he went downstairs until it was over, and that's when he decided to never have children. Men, they supposed to be so strong but cringe when they see childbirth.

As Stacey and the paramedics worked on my mom to try and get her ready for my arrival, my dad stood next to her with emergency supplies and flashlights just in case the lights went out. As she pushed and pushed, the weather got worst. Right towards the end, a tree fell on the house, which knocked a huge hole in the side of the porch, and rain began to pour into our home. When my father went down to check on Uncle Josh, he heard my mother scream out real loud, "Theos!" That's when my father turned around and ran back upstairs. When he reached the top of the stairway, he saw that part of the old oak tree next to their bedroom window had crashed into the bedroom. Stacey raced over to cover the windows while my mother was getting ready to push. That's when the paramedics noticed that my mother's pressure was dropping, and she began to lose a lot of blood.

My dad told me that she was screaming out, "The storm, the storm!" when he finally calmed her down, she whispered to him, "I Love You, God Chaser, keep chasing Him," and then, she stopped breathing.

By then, they had just pulled me out in time when she took her last breath. My mother died while giving birth to me, then the rain ended. When everything was over, they noticed that glass from the windows shattering had pierced my mothers' right side, which had plowed into her lung. No one noticed it because it was already so much blood on the bed. A part of my father's world was destroyed that day, and at the same time, he fell in love with someone he had just met.

"My name is Storm Isabella Chasin, and I am, The Daughter of God."

My father raised me with the help of Stacey and his brother Josh. Stacey taught me all the girly things like hair care, nail care, makeup, how to be a lady, and those special times of the month every woman has. Uncle Josh taught me all the hands-on things and getting my hands dirty, how to put a thermostat in a dodge pickup truck, how to put siding on a two-story house, and how to respectfully watch football. My uncle always told me that it's mandatory to always be a Dallas Cowboys fan for the sake of all humanity. I know now that he was a diehard Cowboys fan because his casket was blue with a Dallas Cowboys star in the inside of the casket, so when you close it, the star would shine on him forever.

Now, my father, I can say so much about that man of God, but then I will take up the rest of your book. My father taught me everything about God and my mother, Mrs. Faith Chasin, and how everything in life just fell into place according to God's plan. The thing with that is, how godly can a person be?

I have lots of stories to tell you, but I will just choose one that I feel would be great access to your book. I can tell you how a woman's life can change from great, to hell, and from hell, to Godly all over a few years' time. A woman can hold so many secrets that it is totally impossible for any man to crack a woman's heart all the way open. I don't know one man that knows everything about his woman. They can say,

"I know everything about my wife, we don't hide secrets from each other, I trust her just like she trusts me."

But as a woman, I know that is not true. Every woman hides certain things from their men, just like men hide stuff from their women. We have some women that live by a need to know basis, don't ask, don't tell. I'm pretty sure some women will discuss the important things, especially if it's life or death, health things, and something important about their children, that's understandable. If a man was to sit his wife down and they have a heart to heart conversation about life, finances, kids, jobs, and so forth, I'm pretty sure it will be something that she is not telling him. As a man, I'm pretty sure it's something that he doesn't tell her. What do men call it? Oh, yeah, the man code. Well, just like the man code that they talk to each other about, we have to woman code. Only one friend knows every little thing about her best friend, especially if she is a true best friend.

The reason I am saying all of this is because women have ways to make a man think that everything is his idea. We can buy stuff and put it in the back of the closet and tell him that they always had that outfit, and they just never had the right time to wear it. Smart women would have a separate bank account that the man never knows about. It's not that she is trying to hide or steal money from her man, but it's called the "What If" account. That means, what if we don't work out and I have to relocate, what if he or I lose our job and we spent all the savings on bills, so we won't be behind until we get another job. What if our things get stolen, and they took everything out of our account, and most of all, what if our children need something and they don't want to tell dad that they need money again, they'll go to mom for it. Oh, and one more, bail money, just in case some stuff jumps off and we go to jail, anything can happen the way this world is today."

Storm laughed and said, "Look at me, I have strayed away from the subject at hand, sorry. We could carry the love of an old boyfriend in our hearts forever, the pain of a broken relationship, the heartache of another family member or friend, and the pain of losing a child or a parent. Our hearts are deep and closed off to the world. If a man says he knows everything about his woman is just fooling himself, they will never know the heart of a woman, especially when she gets mad. That's when you really need to look out and have bail money ready. There is a reason why I am saying all of this about a woman's heart, I am a living witness of secrets of the heart.

When I was 22 years old, I met a guy named Cody Williams. We met in the grocery store one year on Thanksgiving Day. We were standing in this god-awful long line with only one item in our hands. He was standing behind me, holding a bottle of vanilla extract, and I had a pack of pie crust in my hands. As the lines moved slower than father's time, he made a comment and said, "I guess we would be out of her in time for Christmas dinner. We both laughed, and I said, "Nah, maybe we can make it to Thanksgiving dinner by 1997." he laughed even harder. I know that my responses weren't that funny, but it made me blush that someone laughed at my corny jokes. No one ever laughs at my jokes, but my dad and Uncle Josh. I looked at him and noticed that he was a very handsome man. He stood about 6'feet tall, nice chocolate skin, low haircut, and a very lowcut beard. He had on some stonewashed jeans, dark brown timberland boots that weren't laced all the way up. A button-down casual brown striped shirt with a black tank top under it. He had on a brown and tan hat that read "Soldier for Christ" written in white cursive letters. He had on a gold chain necklace with the bracelet to match, blue jeans, and a brown sweater vest. After carefully observing this piece of dark chocolate, I looked down at his hands, no wedding ring. I turned around slowly and closed my eyes and started thanking God in total silence because what I was looking at was nothing but an angel from heaven. If God had angels that looked that good in heaven, then I need to do what I can to get up there.

As the line moved up a bit, I started to think to myself that I need to strike up another conversation with him before it was too late, and I never see him again.

"So, you are out getting last minute things too or like me, getting stuff that the elders of the house ran out of?" He smiled and said, "Actually, I am here from out of town."

Right then, my whole world crashed. He wasn't even from Atlanta, so why try to catch this man? I felt my entire world crash, so I let it go, any chances with him just was shot down because I do not do out of town relationships. He continued to speak,

"I am here with a friend of mine from college, and he invited me to come to dinner at his house. I called to tell him that I made it to Atlanta, and I asked if I could bring anything. Tony told me to bring vanilla extract before his Aunts canceled the entire day. So, here I am, store number five to get the vanilla extract. Never again will I go to a grocery store in ATL on Thanksgiving to get the vanilla extract. I almost lost my religion in the parking lot, trying to get in here. I'm sorry, where are my manners? My name is Cody nice to meet you."

He reached out his hand, and I reached out mine so we could properly introduce each other. "Hello, my name is Storm." At that moment, he looked at me with an expression that almost made me drop those pie crusts and run into his arms. "Your real name is Storm? How unique. I never met anyone with a name like that before. Interesting."

Before I could comment, the cashier said, "Next!" I turned to her with all the rage in my heart because this is one conversation I wanted to continue. I looked at him and said, "Thanks." I turned around and moved forward to check out. We didn't say anything for a minute while I was being checked out. Once the bagger bagged my pie crust, I looked at Cody and said, "Well, it was nice to meet you, Mr. Cody. Have a wonderful holiday." And I walked away. I heard him say, "You to Storm." With the most amazing smile on his face. As I walked to the car, I couldn't get this man off my mind. How could something so handsome be so single? Oh well, I thought to myself, it must be something about him that the reason why he is single.

I finally made it to my grandma's house to help with the cooking. I sat the pie crust on the counter and picked up whatever I saw that needed to be done. The whole time I was in a trance. That dude was beyond fine, he kind of looked like Method Man. You know that thug swag with a little sophistication in it? Hmm... As I began to help everyone place the food on the tables, the men gathered the family together so they could bring everyone to the table. Soon we all sat down, and my dad came over to pray over the food and the family before we could begin. After the prayer was over, my aunt thanked everyone for coming and pitching in for this year's dinner. Then complained that everyone needs to eat slowly because dessert wasn't ready yet.

We all sat down to dinner, and people were still coming into the house with more trays of food. I thought to myself, "How are we going to eat all of this? That's when I realized that we had 20 men here, we won't have leftovers.

We continued to eat and enjoy each other's company. I really loved seeing my dad so happy during the holidays, he really needed this time with family. I got up from the table and went into the kitchen to get more cranberry sauce to put on the table because, for some reason, it kept disappearing. Once I came back into the dining room, I placed the sauce on the table, and when I looked up, there he was. Standing at the dinner table, shaking hands with my dad, it was Cody. My heart raced, my eyes got blurry, and my entire body got hot. Why and how did he get here? As I stared at him, he glanced around the room, and we finally locked eyes on one another. I can tell he was just as shocked as I was to see each other so soon.

My cousin Tony, my aunts son, came into the room and said, "Everyone, this is my best friend Cody Wilkins, we stay together in Nashville, and he didn't have anywhere to go for Thanksgiving, so I asked Uncle Theos could he come to dinner (since he's the eldest here) and he said he never turns a soul away, especially during the holidays. So, here he is."

Everyone said their welcomes and blessings for him coming, until my aunt yelled out, "Is that the one you called to bring me the vanilla extract? If so, he needs to get his tail into this kitchen, so I can finish these pies!" the whole house started laughing, and Tony pushed him into the kitchen. While walking through a house of almost 50 people, Cody shook hands with every family member that they walked past. Then, he was finally standing in front of me. Tony began to introduce us until his mother yelled again, "Extract! Now!" then Tony snatched the vanilla extract out of Cody's hand and ran to the kitchen.

I stood there speechless. Cody smiled and said, "Wow, who would have ever known we would be seeing each other again and at your family's house of all places." He took his hat off and held it in his hands took one foot back and bowed in front of me like I was a queen or something. "Pleasure to meet you again Queen Storm." As he rose up slowly, my cousin Tony came running back into the dining room and grabbed Cody and pushed me. "Cody, Tony said laughing, "that's my cousin Storm, her dad is my uncle Theos and apparently that's his daughter Storm. Watch out, she's a beast and an ugly one at that."

I looked at Tony with an evil smile on my face and said, "Can you excuse me Cody? I have something to do really quick." I turned my head slightly to Tony and before he knew it, I had grabbed him around his neck and put him in a choke hold. Then I turned and put him in a full-Nelson until he screamed bloody murder. The whole house got quiet, they all looked at Tony and I and seen what I was doing to him. Not one word was spoken. For about two minutes, the house was the quietest it had ever been in three days. Then everyone turned back around and continued eating and talking like nothing was going on just a few feet away from them. While I proceeded to shake the life out of my cousin, I overheard my dad say, "She learned that from her Uncle Josh" and he continued eating.

By the time I was done, Tony was laughing and choking on the wall. After he caught his breath, he walked back over to Cody and said, "Hey man, I was kidding, this is my awesome cousin Storm Chasin. You know you have that one cousin that will kick a whole in your back if you ever play with them too much. Well, this is one of them."

Cody laughed and said, "Yeah, I know, we met at the grocery store. I was standing behind her and we had a small conversation about how ridiculous the lines where."

Mrs. Kris, how did that happen? The man I met in the store was standing in my aunts dining room. God has a way of doing things, I felt it was God that made us meet, it was God that had that man in my aunt's house. We never know what God is doing, even though it doesn't make sense to us, it makes perfect sense to Him. Who are we to question God?

As the night continued, Cody and I talked and shared many different things with each other. I told him the story of how my mom died, how I helped my uncle fix a water pump on his coworkers' car, and why I always fought Tony when we were little. He told me about his family and how being the only boy in a house full of girls was horrible. He was the only male in a house of five sisters and his mom. He explained to me the worth of a woman and how he knows our mood swings, that time of the month, heartbreak, and strengths a woman goes through. He told me how he met my cousin Tony and how they became best friends.

As I sat there listening to him, all I could think of was, it must be something about him the reason why he is single. How can a man this fascinating and this fine, be single? I was too busy trying to catch a flaw in his story or any imperfections in his looks to realize that this man sounds 100% perfect. I decided to ask him besides constantly thinking and wondering what his flaws are.

"Cody? May I get you some more pie or something else to drink?" he looked at me with that gorgeous smile and said, "No thank you, but let me take your plate into the kitchen for you because I know you've already done enough today. Would you like for me to bring you something back?" As he began to get up from the table, I felt my heart fall into my stomach. My head started spinning and my breathing changed from slow pace to rapid. I looked at him and said, "I would like a glass of Jack and coke with three cherries." He looked at me and said, coming up my friend."

I smiled and said thank you. Once he was away in the kitchen, I got up from the table and raced to the bathroom to check my makeup and to see if I still looked good after eating dinner. When I was done, I kneeled on the floor in front of the sink and asked God a question. "God? What are you doing? Why is this man so wonderful and why did you put this together? What is your plan? No man on earth can be this wonderful, besides my father. Does this man have a motive, is he a con artist of women, a hustler, an abuser or what? God if this is you doing this, please let me know. Give me a sign or a warning shot or something. Work with me, holla at your girl or something."

After praying to God, I got up and washed my hands and double checked one more time in the mirror to make sure I didn't have any turnip greens stuck in my teeth and that my breath smelt minty fresh. I turned to exit the bathroom, before I turned the knob, I looked up to God and said, "Your will be done, Amen."

I walked back into the dining room and there I saw Cody sitting at the table with Tony and they were laughing and talking amongst each other. I walked over to the table to where they were and leaned down to whispered in Tony's ear. "Get out of my seat you evil fowl beast from the bottom of the earth before I strap you to the bumper of my car and drag you down the street by your feet." He turned and looked at me and said, "See, that's why I hope you trip and fall into a pile of ......"

"Tony! My auntie yelled, "trip over a pile of what?" Tony looked at his mom and said, "A pile of love mom! I was going to say a pile of love!" She looked at him and said, "Umm Hmm, you better have cleaned that up boy, you never too old for a butt whooping, remember that!" He smiled at me with an evil smile and said to his mom, "Yes, ma'am!"

When Tony turned around to look at me, he smiled and said, "You got saved this time, but I'll catch you in the living room for round two, with your bride of chucky looking self." Then he pushed me. One thing I can say about my cousin Tony, he was the best friend and best cousin any one can ask for. We were more like brothers and sisters than we were cousins, and I love him dearly.

That night, I truly believed God heard everything I said to Him in the restroom. Cody was just that guy that comes into a woman's life and sweeps her off her feet. Every woman has that one man in her life that was her prince charming. Every woman has that one man in their life that was perfect in every way and if a woman says they never had that experience then that means he hasn't come yet, or she never recognized him when he was there in her life until it was too late.

As time went on, Cody and I finally became a couple of love birds. The more I was with him the more I fell head over hills for him. I finally realized why Cody was so awesome. He grew up in a house full of women and he experienced firsthand how to treat a woman. He told me he has seen what heartbreak looks like on a woman, he witnessed what love looks like on a woman, betrayal, jealousy, mood swings, struggle, depression, happiness, joy and peace on a woman, and strength of a woman. He told me that all those years living in a house full of women, made him the man that he is today. He told me that when I met him in the grocery store that day, he had gotten out of a two-year relationship with a woman that cheated on him with his former coworker. I thought to myself back then, "How could you cheat on a guy this wonderful? What was that lady thinking?" So, I asked him one day what he did for her to cheat on him?"

He told me that he didn't do anything wrong. He said, "Just like men, women can get greedy too and want more than what God has for them. I spent time with Milla, that's her name, I worked and took care of home, we were engaged, we had a future mapped out for us, we had goals for our life and relationship. We took spontaneous trips out of town sometimes, we played games and pillow fights in the house on rainy days. We, or shall I say I, did what I was supposed to do in a healthy relationship. But where I messed up at was letting my so-called friends come over all the time to watch sports and to just hang out.

Temptation is stronger than what most people think it is. The flesh is weak just like the Bible says. My now ex-best friend, Deadrick, betrayed me and started coming on to her behind my back. He saw how amazing she was and how much love we had for each other and he wanted that. He was dating a woman at the time, but she didn't want to do all the things he had to offer her. She just wanted to hang out in clubs with her friends. She paid more attention to how she looked than she did him. She posted pictures of herself on Facebook every chance she got, like if she was looking for approval or something. She always wore clothes that revealed too much and what she was working with. Don't get me wrong, there is nothing wrong with a woman posting beautiful pictures of herself, but sometimes, every man doesn't need to see what another man's woman is working with all the time because that's when temptation comes in and lust.

I'm not taking up for him or anything but if a person is not happy in a relationship, then be man or woman enough to leave. It might be hard to too, but someone has to do it. Deadrick girlfriend was one of those women that wanted the benefits from a man but not love. He was heads over hills for her. When the relationship got toxic, besides breaking up with her, he cheated on her, with Milla.

Later, after Milla and I broke up, we ran into each other and I offered to take her to lunch so I can see where I went wrong in the relationship. Milla told me that she got caught up in the fact that someone new was interested in her and that the thrill of having an affair was a rush for her. She enjoyed the secrecy. It started off as Deadrick talking to her about how to make his relationship with his girlfriend work and it ended up with them spending time together going to lunch and walks in the park because how distraught he was over his girlfriend not being dedicated, then on thing lead to another and they ended up sleeping together.

My thing about that was why Deadrick didn't come to me and why he picked Milla to fill the hole in his heart. He had a choice between lots of women, but he chose mine. I knew something wasn't right when I started to notice that Milla wasn't interested in the things we use to do, the love making got less and less, and she began to flinch when I hugged her and when I kissed her goodbye before work. But nothing could have prepared me that it was my best friend that was taking up her time. She later apologized and I did the Godly thing and forgave her and Deadrick. It was hard and it took me months to get over it with the strength God gave me, and I didn't date anyone else after that because I didn't want to enter into another relationship with the pain and hurt from the last one. It wouldn't be fair to the next woman."

Storm reached down and grabbed her bottle water and took a drink. While she did that, I decided to do the same thing. Storm put her bottle down and began to talk again. "Mrs. Kris, the reason I am telling you this is because all of it will tie into why I love God. This will not be a tragic story about heartbreak or drama in my life. It's about how God can bring people together out of love. If people would let God take over their life, He will show them that He is doing everything for their good. Yes, it will be good days, it will be bad days, but people have to realize that God don't make mistakes and He don't mess with freewill. He gives us choices, we make good choices, we make bad choices and He is there with us every step of the way.

I heard someone say one time that God has a blueprint for our lives, and we won't understand it until the project is finished. My father always told me that how much he loved my mother, but God loved her more and He wanted her with Him for a reason. He said one day, "I don't know why God called her home so soon. It's not my place to question God. But I do believe that every little thing happens for a reason and no one on this earth can tell me it doesn't. Yes, I was mad at God for taking my wife and mother of my child from this earth. But as I went on, I knew He had His reasons. I'll ask Him when I get there."

My dad raised me the best he could. I only seen him freak out one time in my life and that's when I became a woman and started my menstrual cycle for the first time at the age of 13. I never seen a man panic that much before in my life. He ran next door and got my Aunt Stacey and told her what was going on and he was freaking out like I was dying or something, it was so funny! Auntie Stacey came over and took me to the store and made sure I had pain medicine and the proper things I need during this time in my life. That day when I went downstairs, I saw her in the kitchen with my dad talking to him about it and giving him a cup of water. When I walked into the kitchen, all I heard was, "She's becoming a woman now Theos, maybe she can lay off some of the duties you and Josh be teaching her. It's time to start talking about boys and how her body is about to change." When I heard that, I saw my dad put his head on the table and say, "Why Lord? Not now, I'm not ready!" It was funny because I didn't know rather to laugh or go comfort my father. But leave it up to my Auntie, she did both.

Mrs. Kris, I truly believe that every girl needs a father, males need one too, but a girl needs a father in their life. Rather it be a stepdad, a granddad, or an uncle. Every girl needs a father figure in her life. Knowing that you have a protector, a comforter, and a teacher to be there when she needs them can change how a lot of women grow mentally in life.

I give all the credit to God. I am blessed to have had God, my dad, Uncle Josh, Cousin Tony, and Cody in my life. Every girl needs to experience love from a father figure. Take the positive things that they teach you and apply it to your life and others who didn't have a father figure and pay it forward. Women are powerful creature and we all need to embrace that feeling. If women only knew how much pull they have in the world, but so many of us are caught up in the wrong things. Some of us are caught up in looks, reputation, money, men, working, and trying to prove that we don't need a man to make us happy all the time. Many women can argue my statement but what does every woman want? We want love, love can make you go crazy, it can heal, it can comfort, it can be supportive, and it can kill. Women have to choose which love type of love they want.

I know one lady that is very power driven, her name is Ms. Powell. When I mean power driven, I mean she had to be in control of every aspect of her life. Her job, her friends, and her personal life. She is a CEO of a very well-known company here in ATL and everyone scattered when they saw her coming. No one moved until she said they could, her own friends had to make an appointment just to see her or speak to her. She has it all, the house, the car, the wardrobe, the attitude, the money and the power. I had a conversation with her one day and I asked her if she really happy with her life. She told me yes, so I asked her what her secret was.

This is what she said, "I don't have a secret Storm. I want what I want, and I'll do what I need to do to get it. I wanted to make sure my son and I will be taken care of for the rest of our lives. I don't need a man to take care of me, to love me, or to provide for me. I can do it all myself and that's how I was raised and that's how I live. I gave my heart to a man one time and that's how I got Anthony, my son. I vowed never again to give my heart to a man if it's not my son. It only takes one time for a person to mess over my life and my heart, once you do that, then I'll cut you off."

After she said what she said, I asked her another question, I asked her did she forgive Anthony's father. That answer was very short, all she said was, "No."

"You see Mrs. Kris, what I learned over the years that we can block our own blessings because we won't forgive others. How do you expect to be forgiven by God if you don't forgive the ones who hurt you? Don't you think we all hurt God's feelings on a daily basis? We hurt God more than we hurt each other and yet He still forgives us. No matter the situation, He still forgives us. But He will discipline us just like we would discipline our own kids, but that too is out of love. So, I asked myself, how could this lovely woman be blessed with so many things, but won't forgive one man? Ms. Powell told me the only good thing that came out of that relationship was Anthony, and I totally agree with her. Anthony is a fine young man, even though we fight like cats and dogs, he still is a wonderful person."

When Storm said that, I got confused really quick. Who is Ms. Powell and if she is so vicious like folks think she is, how and why is Storm so close to her? Also, is Anthony an old friend of hers and why would this lady even tell Storm all these things about her life? As I sat there contemplating on if I should ask or just let her talk, I noticed that Storm was staring at me. Creepy.

"Mrs. Kris, I noticed you have a confused look on your face. Is there something you don't understand? You can ask me anything, I'm totally comfortable answering all questions you may have. I did agree to be in your book, so ask away."

I sat up in the chair and readjusted myself. "Ok, Storm, I'm sorry but as I was listening, I was just wondering about your relationship with Ms. Powell and Anthony. If you said her own friends had to have an appointment just to speak to her or see her, how is it that you could be with her and talk to her so freely? If people scatter when she comes around, how is it that she is willing to tell you her deepest secrets and why she doesn't want a relationship anymore? I don't have to put this in the book if you do not want me to, it can be off the record."

"No, Mrs. Kris, it is perfectly fine that you write this down. You have my permission to write down everything. See, Ms. Powell's full name is Ms. Stacey Powell and her son name is Tony, Anthony Powell, is his full name, but you heard me call them Auntie Stacey and Cousin Tony. Ms. Powell was there when I was born. Stacey isn't my real Auntie; she was our neighbor and my moms' best friend. Tony really isn't my cousin, but we grew up together and since our moms were best friends long ago, her son became my cousin since we all were so close, and she helped my dad and uncle raise me.

When Storm told me that, my mouth dropped. I should have known it when she said she use to fight with Anthony like cats and dogs. Tony is short for Anthony; I just never would have put that together because she spoke of Ms. Powell as a power-hungry woman that demands perfection and a beast at work. People amaze me all the time, you never know anyone's story until you take the time out to talk to them and get to know them on another level. That's when I realized that the purpose of this book was deeper than I thought.

We walk around every day and we have no idea about the next person standing next to us. That's why I wanted to write this book, to hear and see the stories of other people. We judge others too quickly and don't take the time out to get to know one another. People that smile everyday could be battling demons on the inside, but they use their poker faces and makeup to cover up the truth. When I was a little girl, an older woman told me that I was "The Seeker". I had no idea what that meant and when I asked her, she told me I would find out what that means when I get older. Years later, another older woman told me the same thing, that I was a seeker. So, when I got home to my computer, I googled the word seeker, and this is what I found.

"The Seeker - a person who is attempting to find or obtain something. "a tenacious seeker of the truth"

WHEN I READ THAT, I KNEW THEN THAT THOSE WOMEN WERE right. All my life I wanted to know

THE TRUTH ABOUT EVERYTHING AROUND ME. I ALWAYS SAW TWO sides to everything and researched as much as I could when I had the chance. Seeking truth and knowledge is a lifelong thing, you could never stop learning and exploring the world and other possibilities.

As Storm readjusted herself in her seat, she continued with her story. "Remember earlier when we started that a woman's heart is deep, and it holds many secrets? Well let me explain why I said that.

After thanksgiving, Cody and I stared seeing each other more and more. Yes, he lived out of town at the time but the more we talked, the more we hung out, he decided to move to Atlanta to be closer to me. He got a job working as a Director, of Network Operations at a well-known Pharmaceutical company while I continue to be a family counselor. I have never been as happy as I am with him, he is truly a God send. Everyone loved the fact that we are together, my dad and Auntie Stacey kept saying how happy they are for us and that my mother would be so proud of me. My dad said that my mother asked God to send Cody to me so I can be happy and experience the love that her and my dad had for each other.

My family compared me and Cody to my mom and dad so much that it scared me. It scared me to the point that I felt that my fate was going to be like my moms, so, Cody and I never had kids. If Cody and I relationship was so much like my dad's and my mom's, why in all of creation would I try to have kids? If our relationship was so alike, did that mean that I would die like my mother did when she was giving birth to me? I didn't want to chance it, so Cody and I talked about it and we decided not to have children no time soon.

The more and more I spent time with Cody, the less I seen Tony. I didn't understand why he slowly disappeared out of our lives. Cody was his best friend and Tony was mine. Every time I asked Auntie Stacey about Tony, she would say he's out of town or he was busy at work. My dad told me one day that he thinks Tony is being distant because Cody might not feel comfortable around us since Tony and I grew up together and we play fight all the time. He said that Tony knows me better than any man, even my dad, because we told each other secrets to one another, we cried together, we fought bullies in school together, we took up for each other and even lied for each other when we were growing up.

My dad said that it's a man thing. When friends get into a serious relationship, men are supposed to make time for your spouse and make time for your friends, you never mix them too together, that's how affairs start. That's why Tony never came around after Cody moved to ATL. My dad said that when a man loves a woman and they get serious, the man is to slow down on the hanging out with the fellas. He can have guy night on weekends or during football season and basketball season, or whatever sports they all love, but a man should never spend more time with his friends than he does his woman.

Woman aren't too quick to cheat on a man she loves unless he is lacking in two departments of a relationship, time and attention. That's really all a woman wants. If you handle those two things with a woman, you will never have to worry about her stepping out on you. But, if you start to put those two things aside or lack in those departments in a relationship and she has mentioned it to you multiple times and nothing has changed, that's when a man needs to worry. That goes for men too, if a woman doesn't have time or attention for her man and he has mentioned it multiple times, then he will step out on her.

It takes a lot for a woman to cheat on her man if she really loves him. My dad said it is five warning signs that women give to let you know that you are slipping in your relationship,

1. **The talk**- she will explain her issues and you and her will talk about it to resolve the problem.
2. **Appearance**- She will start looking and dressing up more to gain your interest so you and her can put the spark back into the relationship.
3. **Readiness**- When you get home from work, she will have

everything done already so he won't have to do anything so she can spend more time with you.

4. **Different ways of Love Making-** She will try new and fun things to gain your attention in the bedroom. Lingerie, shoes, music, and so forth.

5. **Attention** – She will find new and exciting things you can go do as a couple, she will even sit down and watch sports with you, she will do things you like to do just so she could spend more time with her man.

If she has done those five things and nothing has changed, trust me, she will either break it off, or she will stay with the man and find her attention elsewhere. The biggest clue a man should notice about his woman is, after the talks, after the appearance change, the different ways of love making, the readiness, and doing things that you want to do has passed and she starts to show no interest in anything, she's not talking about your relationship anymore and begins to not care if you hang out with the fellas, that's when a man should worry, BIG TIME! She has put her attention and time on something else, or someone else.

"It's funny because my dad is a very wise man and he taught me well, especially in the relationship area. But I truly believe that a person must go through stuff in order to teach about stuff. As far I knew, my dad was the smartest man in the world."

After Storm made that last comment, I noticed her whole facial expression changed. It amazes me how our facial expressions and our eyes can tell a story better than our mouths can. People tell me all the time, why I look like that when someone said something or did something crazy. A person can hold their tongues for a lot of things, but that facial expression isn't going anywhere. I personally have gotten into deep conversations and arguments just by my facial expression, especially when I raise my right eyebrow. When that happens, my family knows that something horrible is about to come out my mouth and everyone should run and hide, so I was told.

As I sat there waiting on Storm to continue with her story, I noticed that she had one tear come down her cheek. I didn't want to ask her why she was tearing up, so I sat there. If she wanted me to know, she would tell me, or it could have been something personal.

"Mrs. Kris, a woman's heart is bigger than a galaxy of stars, we love, and we love hard. The love of a woman is the greatest love any person can get besides the love of God. Man, woman, and child has experienced the love of a woman at some point in their life. Rather it be a grandma, an aunt, sister, cousin, best friend, a teacher, and so forth, every person has felt it. When they feel love given, they don't want to let go. God has instilled a type of love in women that would make the strongest man weak, a ruthless man cringe, and would make the weakest man strong. So how is it that we can love like that and still have room for more love?"

"A year later, Cody and I moved in together in a nice two-bedroom apartment in downtown Atlanta. It was close to both of our jobs, so it made the commute a lot better, especially in Atlanta. With our busy schedule, Cody and I made sure we arranged date night every Friday night, hung with our friends on Saturday night, worshipped God together on Sundays, then ended our weekend with dinner and a movie. I enjoyed being with him, he made my heart flutter every time we were together. He would do things just to keep our love interesting and new. I never known love like this, and I wanted to keep it. But it was still a small hole in my heart that for some reason, was still empty."

A few years past and Cody and I were stronger than ever. I remember the time when I met his sisters and they told me that Cody always talked about me and how much he loved me. Even his mom said I was the best thing that ever happened to him after all he went through with his first marriage. Then she told me that his ex-wife was still with his best friend and now he is cheating on her with her best friend and she knows it but does not want to admit to herself that he is. Love is powerful and deadly if you don't know how to use it.

My uncle Josh told me one time that love is like water, I never understood what he meant by that. He used to talk about love every time we were together. One day, when I was 18 years old, I asked him. It was the day I helped him build a tree house for one of our neighbors across the street from my home. Mr. Tuggle, one of my dads' good friends, asked if Uncle Josh could build a tree house for his grandkids that were coming for the summer and he wanted it to be made like a cottage in the trees. So, Uncle Josh told him that he would be happy to build it for him and we got started right away. This particular day, I decided to ask Uncle Josh why he always talked to me about love and why he referred it to water. This is what he said, ...

"Storm, love is like water, it flows back and forth, spins in circles, crystal clear, and makes you feel good when you have it. At the same time, water can heal you, save you from dehydration, (meaning heat, excessive activity, insufficient fluid consumption, excessive sweating, or medication side effects.) it can refresh you, and can also kill you. Just like we all need water in our life, we need love in our lives as well." He said,

"Go to the grocery store and walk down the aisle with the water bottles. Pay attention to how many different types of bottle water you see. Notice that different companies' sale different types of water. You have sparkling water, vitamin water, flavored water and so forth, right? Some taste better than the others, but it's up to the consumer which one to pick. So basically, you would have to try a few just to see which one you like so you will know which one you would be using from now on or until you find a new one that taste just as better, then, you will just stick to that one, just like you would when you are in love.

Some people don't like the taste of water so they would buy those little packs of flavor aids to put in their waters just like you do. You know you need the water in your diet and in your life, so you find ways to cope with drinking it, so you'll add flavor. Now, think about what I said about water, and see if it doesn't match up with the same views of love.

Would you offer someone muddy water? It doesn't look to appealing and there is no telling what's floating in it, so, you would throw it away and find clean water. See, some people have muddy water in their lives so they would find ways to clean that water because they don't want to stop getting the water from the place where muddy water flows, they afraid to search for better water in a toxic environment. Then, you have people who will filter their water, no matter how safe the water can be, they still want to be sure it is filtered for safety and quality reasons. No matter what they do to filter that water, it is never good enough. So, what about the people who wants to much water? Well, it can also cause health problems, you can be Overhydrated, (meaning, drinking too much water can be dangerous. Overhydration can lead to water intoxication) many people don't realize that. When you get a chance Storm, research it and you will see that I'm right. That's why I said water can kill you and save you, drinking too much water and being in too much water can drown you. A person can be so overwhelmed by water that it would literally kill them. Same as love, a person can be so overly in love with someone that it could kill them. Suicide, ex-lover's revenge, and depression from a breakup to the point a person would stop eating, sleeping and caring for their bodies. Love can have a person's mind Overhydrated and intoxicated, just like water."

"I loved my Uncle Josh's ways of putting things, it always made since and he would say things that would make your views of things clearer and more understandable. I wish he was here four years ago when my life changed, I needed him to explain things to me in what I was feeling and why I had that empty whole in my heart. But I soon found out why everything in my life turned around and made a 360."

Storm got up from her seat and went into the kitchen. While she did that, I gathered my things together and made sure I had enough space left in my recorder and enough ink in my pen for any more notes that I need to jot down. When she returned, she had a tray of Bruschetta with tomato and basil, with another tray of miniature buffalo chicken egg rolls. It looked delicious and I thanked her for the appetizers.

She finally sat down, and she began to speak. "Mrs. Kris, it will be certain things that we will discuss that should not be in the book, but I would still like to tell you."

I looked over at her and said, "Yes ma'am, you have my word that it will not appear in this chapter. Also, the documents you to signed for this book would have it on record." "Thanks" she said.

As we took a little break and began to have lunch, I felt that what she was about to tell me was going to be one of the most interesting stories I have heard so far while creating this book. She has my word that what she will say would be stricken from this chapter and I will take whatever she tells me to the grave. While we ate, she asked me how I was doing and how was the family. We chatted a while and she wanted to know what the inspiration for the book was and how she felt that this book would help so many women and even men because it would help them understand their woman better and to prove that everyone has a story to tell. Then she asked me could she pray over me to ask God to make this book powerful in His name and to help inspire people. I said sure, and we continued lunch.

After lunch was over and we relaxed and cleared our minds. She went and poured me a glass of wine and we sat back at the table in her office at her home.

"Everything in a person's life is usually not what it seems. People will never tell the world exactly what goes on behind closed doors. Yes, a person might be rich and have everything they ever wanted, but behind closed doors, you have to ask yourself are they really happy. A smile is a mask that we all wear sometimes to let people know that things are okay or to show the world that they have their lives in order. A friend of mine calls it our "Poker Face", but at the same time, she thinks everyone is fake but her."

"You see, the whole reason I went so much into detail about certain things is because my life was about to change in an instant. I am going to tell you the short version so you can put it in your book, but when the part I don't want you to put in your book is the whole breakdown of why things turned out like they did in my life. "

Soon as she said that, two young girls burst through the doors and said, "Hi Mom!! Where back from our camping trip! We had so much fun! You should have been there!" One of the little girls came up and hugged Storm and said, "Mom, being in the wilderness is not what it's cracked up to be, I couldn't get any reception on my cell phone out there. The only thing I got out there were mosquito bites and a starring match with a deer that kept trying to come eat all the food, but dad and Uncle Willie kept him away. Please mom, next year when you want alone time, can you please just go to the Bahamas with your friends or something and let us stay home?" The girl laughed and gave her mom a kiss on the forehead and continued upstairs.

Storm laughed and said, "Meet my girls, Faith and Cody, they were on a weekend camping trip with their dad and his brother so I could get some alone time and be able to get my thoughts together before you got here. I thought they were coming back later tonight but I guess I miscalculated their travel time. Once every two months, my husband takes the girls on some kind of wild adventure so I can take time to myself. With me being a counselor, I deal with other people's problems and sometimes what they tell me breaks my heart or overwhelms me, so, he lets me have a stress-free weekend. Once every two months."

The door swung open in the living room and two males walked

through the door laughing and carrying sleeping bags and luggage. They put the luggage down in the living room and walked over to us. One guy sat down in the recliner and the other one reached over to Storm by the hand and made her get up and then gave her a huge kiss. "I've missed you so much baby" he said, "I hope you got plenty of rest while we were gone?" She smiled and said I sure did honey, thank you."

While me and the other guy sat there, he decided to speak and said, "Eww... I think I just threw up a bit in my mouth. Get a room you two." The man that was holding Storm turned and said, or, you can go get the rest of the stuff out the car and let me embrace my wife. That's why you look like a deer in headlights with your ugly self." They both laughed and he walked over to Storm and said, "If my brother comes up missing, I swear I won't tell the police anything, hint hint." Storm smiled and said, before you go outside, let me introduce you to Mrs. Kris, she is the one I told you both about that was coming over and I was going to be in her new book. Mrs. Kris, this is Kenneth, my husbands' brother and this, is my husband, Tony."

When she said that, my heart started racing, my breathing slowed down, my mouth got dry, my voice started cracking and my eyes got bigger than an owl's eyes. Before I knew it, I yelled out, "What the hell!?" I was so embarrassed when I said that, I had to apologize for my outburst. "Oh My Gosh, I'm so sorry Storm, I didn't mean to say that, I meant to say, Hello. Please forgive me."

Everyone laughed and said it was okay. Tony walked over to me and shook my hand and said, "I guess she didn't get to that part of her story yet. Well, just wait, it's coming." I reached over and shook Tony's hand and apologized again for my unprofessional outburst.

"Mrs. Kristina, it's okay, trust me, please, continue your evening. I might sit in with you guys once I get the girls settled and send my brother off on his way. It was nice to finally meet you ma'am."

I released his hand and said, "Nice to meet you too Tony." Then I sat down with a dazed and confused look on my face. Storm kissed Tony one more time and said, "We'll be here baby, take your time getting the girls together and unpack." He turned to her and said, "I'll check on the girls and let Kenney out and I'll be back in here, I don't want to miss this." Then he walked away.

Storm sat there for a minute to let me collect my thoughts because I was scatter brain at the moment. I took another big sip of wine then put the glass back down. Storm laughed and said, "I'll go get the other bottle of wine just in case we need it for later. Also, I'll bring you a cup of water to help you get over the shock of what just happened." When she said that, all I could do is think about the story her Uncle Josh told her about the water, that made me feel even more light-headed. Lord have mercy! I had to ask the Lord what he was doing in my life, how was I able to come across such amazing, unique, and mysterious women? The only thing I heard in the back of my mind was, **"Everything is for a reason and a season."** Was that God telling me that or did my mind just slip from the shock? I did not see this coming, was Tony her hole in her heart? Was not being with Cody the emptiness she was feeling? Where did her daughters come from? I was trying to analyze her time frame that she has told me, and it seems like things weren't adding up. Maybe that's the part that she wants me to keep off the record, I don't know what to expect with this one.

By the time Storm came back, I was literally sitting there looking over my notes I had taken down while she was telling me her story, I couldn't find anything that could have given me a clue about her and Tony. Except the part where she found out that he wasn't really her cousin and her auntie wasn't really her aunt. Besides that, I couldn't see anything that even came close to what I just witnessed.

When she came back into the living room, Tony was coming downstairs and walked over to the couch to sit next to Storm. "So", he said, what have I missed?" Storm looked over at him and said, "Really dude? You just going to plop down on the couch and say what have you missed? You missed a lot, but I'm glad you're here so we can tell her how things happened." He turned to her with a look on his face that I couldn't make out. Was it fear? Was it confusion? Or was it a look of why haven't you told her yet? I didn't want to stare at the man, so I just looked down and acted like I was looking for my pen even though it was in my hand.

"Mrs. Kris, Storm said, now is the time where we strike what I'm about to say from the records." When she said that, I said, "Okay, let me turn off the tape recorder and put my pen down. Let's look over our contract really quick so you would know that what you tell me will be stricken from the book. Also, since Tony is here, I will need him to sign one as well so if anything happens or if he decides to add to your story and put his input in anything, he will be covered too." As I pulled out Storm privacy contract, I asked him to read over it and sign it under her name. After I put away all my things, she began to speak.

Tony looked over at me and said, "I don't know how you women chit chat with each other, but you have my permission to put the ending in your book." Storm smiled at me and said, "Yes, please do. You can sum up what we are about to tell you, but we don't want to put all the details in the book because no one would truly understand. Let's begin."

AFTER ABOUT TWO HOURS OF THEM TELLING ME EVERYTHING, I sat there in amazement. What I just heard was the most inspiring, saddest, and shocking thing I had ever heard. The reason for the water and love story was clearer, the emptiness that Storm had felt was revealed, the love of a father was proven, and how a woman's heart being stronger and more complex than a man's heart was explained. Now, I see why they didn't want it in the book even though I knew a lot of people, men and woman, could relate to their story. I was baffled, speechless, and at the same time honored that they entrusted me with this testimony. My heart was filled with every emotion that a human being could possibly feel. Love, joy, hurt, sadness, guilt, shame, anger, surprised, and fear of the unknown was rushing my body all at the same time.

Love can be so beautiful at times. The heart wants what the heart wants and who are we to tell our hearts what and who we should and shouldn't love at the end of the day. No matter how hard we try to fight it, Love really is like water, it can kill us and make us stronger. The secrets of the heart can only be explained by God, He is the one who gave us love. God is the one who showed us that love can outstand the worst parts of our lives and loving each other is one of the things God wants us to do, love and forgive. God showed the world the greatest love any person can give when He gave us His son, Jesus Christ, to save humanity. Sacrifice was His gift, forgiveness was His love, and patience is His reward. Jesus love flows through us like water. Now how can you argue with that?

I am forbidden to tell you what was said during the last part of our meeting, but I do have permission to tell you the outcome of Storms testimony. After everything was said and done, this is how Storm ended her testimony.

"You see Mrs. Kris, the man who I thought was my uncle, really was my father, my dad, Theos, didn't care that my mother was unfaithful to him, he raised me as his daughter anyway. My dad felt that no matter what, a girl needs her father and just so happen I had two fathers. Cody was the love of my life, but Tony was my true love and Cody's best friend, that's why we named our first daughter Cody.

My auntie reasons for adopting Kenneth was explained, the love for Tony was explained and the breakup with Cody was explained. Don't get me wrong, Cody is, and will always be a wonderful man, but he just wasn't what my heart wanted in the end. Please remember what we told you and keep it locked in your heart forever. My father, Theos, is the strongest man I know, and Josh was the wisest man I knew. Put them all together with everything that I told you and you will see why a "storm" has so much rain inside it. The water from the storm helped everything heal, for it to grow bigger and stronger than before. I don't regret any parts of my life, and I thank God every day for how it turned out."

My name is Storm Isabella Chasin-Powell, and I am, The Daughter of God.

CHAPTER 4
TREASURE POSSESSION

"I would like to start my story by saying that Jesus is everything to me. If it wasn't for His grace, I would be dead already. Jesus can block anything in your life when you give yourself to Him. I know so many people that would say Jesus has brought them out of the darkest times in their lives and I know some that will say Jesus was never there for them. I'm here to clear up some confusion about the way God loves us, and I hope that this testimony will help someone struggling with what to believe in a world full of chaos.

The devil comes in many shapes and forms. He could appear as pretty as a rainbow, charming, manipulative, cunning, hypnotizing being and as deadly as a scorpion's venom. The devil is only out for one thing, your soul. In life, we are faced with obstacles where we question God's judgement. We all must understand that God will never do anything to hurt or harm His children. In the bible, John 14:30 Jesus Christ mentioned that the devil was the prince of this world and he had no hold over Him. As much as we try to keep the devil out of our lives and live a sin free life, the devil will find a way in to try and destroy us or rip your family apart. He is a very devious being. The devil is always in character, disguising himself as the light, the way out, whispering in our ear to do wrong, and to deceive us in every way he can. I hate to say it, but we've all have fallen under his spell plenty of times in our lives and he won't stop until he has us. That's why prayer is so important.

People now-a-days try to get rich quick and will do anything to have a lot of money and show the world that they are not poor. We want materialistic things for two reasons, to show off what we have to the world, so people will think we rich, or we get things to see what our hard work and determination can bring us so we can sit back and say, "I did this." This generation we in today feels that they all can get rich and ball out like the rappers they see on TV, or if they shake their bottoms half naked on TV or on social media for likes, they can get famous. But what about the ones who are working towards something positive in their lives? What do we say about them? Nothing, we are silent to the positive things because no one wants to hear about it, especially the media. It goes unnoticed and unheard of to the world, and why is that? Because the world revolves around drama, we hate to be in it, but we love to watch it on TV and social media.

My point in saying all of this is because we have to know the difference between good and evil doings. My mother always said, "If it doesn't feel right, then it's a possibility that it ain't right." That gut feeling will never lead you wrong. That little voice in your head will always tell you the truth. She always said that little voice in your head was God telling you not to do something or go another way. Think about it Mrs. Kris, how many times have you heard that voice in your head telling you not to do something and you do it anyway? Then when you don't do what that little voice told you not to do, the first thing you think of is, "I should have followed my first mind." Well, that first mind is God, but people fail to realize that or don't want to accept it. Life is funny like that.

I want to tell you about a time when I came face to face with the devil himself. It was last year around this time in April that I met a person that I adored very much. It was a young lady, let's call her Abigail for your book purpose, I know we can't use real names. I love my name you gave me in your book, Treasured Possession, I will take that to the grave with me, Thank You."

Before we continued, Treasure walked over to her TV remote and turned the TV off. She reached down and grabbed and old photo album that was under her entertainment center and started flipping through the pictures. For a moment, I wondered if she forgot that I was in the room because she was singing at the same time while looking through the album. Just as I got ready to say something to her, she stopped. She was fixed on one particular photo that made her eyes water and her voice crack.

"Mrs. Kris, what I about to show you is the reason I said I met the devil face to face. Remember when I said the devil comes in all shapes and forms and can be as pretty as a rainbow? Well meet Abigail Tucker, or Abby for short. Who says the devil always had to come as a man? He can disguise himself as a woman too."

I reached out my hand to grab the picture from Treasure. When I grabbed it, she took a deep breath and released her hand from the picture. I glanced at the picture and I couldn't believe my eyes. It was a young lady with hazel green eyes, long flowing burgundy and black hair, maybe about 5'4 with a slim shape to her. She was an African American woman, about 25 or 26 years old with a honey brown complexion. Her skin glowed like the sunset in the morning and her smile would hypnotize any person that would come in contact with her. In the photo, she had on a pink t-shirt that read, "Bewitched with Love" and it was written in gold glitter letters in cursive. She wore a pair of dark ripped stonewashed blue jeans and on her feet were pink converse tennis with white shoestrings. On her left arm she had on a gold watch trimmed in diamonds and a tattoo on her right arm that read, "Unbothered" in bold letters.

As I looked at this picture, all I could wonder was, why is Treasure calling this woman the devil? But then I realized something. While I was in process of writing this book, things are never as they seem. Looks can really be deceiving. As I continued to look over this picture, I saw a young man holding her hand. He was a very handsome young man. He was medium built, maybe 5'11 mocha colored young man maybe in his early twenties. Nicely built individual, you can tell he works out, he had medium length black and blonde dreads that reached to his shoulders. He was wearing a black t-shirt, black jogging pants with the word "Chosen" written down the side of his right pants leg and black and white tennis shoes on. On his right arm, it seems like he had a tattoo of some kind of animal. I couldn't tell if it was a lion or a black panther, but whatever it was, I could tell it was very detailed. After looking at the photo, I looked over at Treasure and she was just staring at me. I was a bit creeped out, but I was too focused on the fact that she called this beautiful young lady the devil.

"Treasure?" I said in confusion, this is the young lady you called the devil. Abigail? She looks so harmless and sweet, and the man holding her hand looks very happy to be with her." As Treasure leaned over to take the picture back, she took a deep breath and said, "Mrs. Kris, the devil is like a noun, he can disguise himself as a person, place, or thing in this world, rather it be a person or a thing, if he wants your soul and your sanity, he would stop at nothing to get it. That bastard can trick the weakest and the smartest person on earth to fall for his schemes. I always told my son, never trust anyone who smiles all the time, if it is too good to be true, then probably it isn't. Sit back Mrs. Kris, let me introduce to you, the devil himself."

When she said that, all I could do is pray in silence, I've seen those movie's where a person said that and it didn't end well for that person, well this isn't a movie. I am not that little girl that always gets possessed in those movies and die at the end. I am not the person that sits around a wait to get murdered trying to go look for the strange noise that is coming out the back room and trying to go see whatever that dark figure is sitting in the corner. WE! Don't do that! When people say crazy stuff like that, we remove ourselves from the situation and move on with our lives. I got too much to do then be sitting here waiting and wondering what's going to happen next. As I sat there getting ready to gather my things, I thought to myself, "What the hell she means by, "Let me introduce to you the devil himself?" I don't want to see him; she can have all of that! He can stay exactly where he at and leave me the alone."

As I started putting my tape recorder away and gathering my papers to put back in my briefcase, Treasure stopped me and said, "Mrs. Kris, don't go please, I have to tell you why I agreed to tell my testimony, this will help a lot of mothers and fathers to watch the company they children keep around them. If I would have watched and prayed like I supposed to, none of this would have happened and I could still have my son."

When she said that, and I saw the tears begin to form, a part of me was like, "Let her email me her testimony" and the other part of me heard a voice say, "I am protected by the blood of Jesus, stay" so, I stayed.

"Abigail is every man's dream, she is beautiful, charming, respectful, educated, and very manipulative, and my son, Dylan loved her. He met her at the mall one day while shopping for a birthday gift for me about a year ago. When he came home that day, he was so excited, he felt that she was going to be his wife one day. My son Dylan or DJ for short, has always been infatuated by love, he use to always say that he wanted a marriage like his dad and I. Dylan Sr., my husband, taught DJ everything he knew about life, love, money, and how to be a great father. The only thing my husband fell to teach him was how to keep his room clean. I don't know what it is about guys, but their cars would look amazing inside and out, but that bedroom would always look like pure hell.

Anyway, DJ and Abby started dating for a while before we actually met her. His father always told him not to bring every girl you date around your family, especially if the relationship is only for a season. He told him, "If the relationship is just a fling, then let it be a fling, but never tell or show everyone everything about you until it's time. If you are dating someone for just a few months, that person shouldn't know where your parents stay, your middle name, where you hang out the most, what you like to do in your downtime at home. Share enough information with them so if they become a stalker or obsessed with you, they won't have much to go on because you will keep them at a distance son. Your mom is a wonderful and powerful woman. Still, she will shut any person down quick if they ever crossed her or hurt anyone in her family. Your mother knows how to read people very well, and that's why I say don't bring any and every female you date around your mother because she will let you know if that person is good or bad or not. Why do you think I only have two best friends? Your mother told me that the people I kept around me was not good and later I found out she was right. One friend ended up cheating on his wife with her sister and they mom and the other person I hung around was a backstabber and your mom peeped all of that. So, listen to her when she says certain things, she's not nagging, she just knows." He told DJ, "When a woman has a baby, God gives them certain abilities that only women can get, I never knew what it was, and I don't know how to explain it, but they have it."

"Dylan Sr. is a man of grace and courage, God Himself gave me Dylan, I couldn't ask for anything more. I love him, thirty-five years of marriage and never once have I ever thought of being with anyone else. People have their flaws, but God has their hearts. He will be here later today, he went to go visit someone for a few hours and if you still here, you will be able to meet him."

I glanced at Treasure with a smile and said, "It would be an honor ma'am."

"Well back to my story, after about six months or so, DJ asked his dad could he introduce Abby to us. His father was hesitant about it, he said wait another month before you bring her around your mom and I. DJ told him that Thanksgiving was approaching. She didn't have nowhere to go for the holidays, and he would like to bring her by for us to meet her, so it won't be so occurred on thanksgiving day. My husband came home and discussed it with me, and I finally gave in. I had heard so much about her and he had been spending so much time with her, it felt like I already knew so much about her. We've seen pictures of her he had in his phone and watched as my son changed over the past six months. He was happy all the time, he spent so much time with her that for a second, he stopped coming over for Sunday dinners. In my house, family always come together for Sunday dinner. Always!

One day DJ called and said they would be over around 6pm and that he would call when they were on the way. He was so happy to finally let us meet her, I didn't know who was excited the most, him or his dad. My husband was talking about grandbabies and having the chance to build tree houses and birthday parties and everything. DJ is the only child and when we had him, Dylan worked a lot and was only able to spend time with him on weekends and just a little time with him at night. When DJ became a thirteen, Dylan thought it was time to start teaching him how to be a man, so he started his own business remodeling house and he took DJ with him as much as possible and even paid him wages just like a regular employee. By the time DJ was eighteen, he had already had $25, 000 in his own bank account and his own car. Every young boy needs a real father or a father figure in their lives. I'm pretty sure you've heard that before."

I looked at her and said, "Yes, a few women that I have interviewed has said the same thing. So, it must be true, and I totally agree." Then she said, "Amen."

"Anyway, we finally met Abby and she was everything that DJ said she was. She was beautiful, kind, respectful and most of all very lady like. I didn't have any complaints about her. She came for thanks-giving and he showed her off to everyone. He told his cousins that she was Mrs. Possession and that they were going to be married one day. He was the happiest I have ever seen. One day, they both came to the house to have Sunday dinner and DJ cousin Linda was there. She had flown in from New York to go to a conference here in Memphis that her job sent her too. That day was a little different than others. I noticed some things that I had never seen before and that's when the red flags came. DJ was sitting in the living room talking to Linda and I noticed that Abby was staring at Linda in a strange way. DJ and Linda were talking about old times, laughing and such, Abby began to feel a little uneasy. I sat back and watched for a minute because what I was feeling, I wanted to make sure it was correct. Linda got up from the couch to go get a drink of water and DJ stayed seated until she came back. Once Linda was out the way, I grabbed Linda and said, "Don't go back in there just yet, I want to see what's about to happen." Linda looked at me and said, "What do you mean, what's about to happen? What's going on?" I didn't say nothing back to Linda and I continued to watch. As I suspected, Abby walked over to DJ and said something to him, and DJ facial expression changed. Whatever she said to him, he didn't like it. He got up from the couch and walked away. Abby sat down where DJ was sitting and started smiling. My first thought was she was ready to go, and he wasn't ready, then my second thought was, apparently, she don't know what type of family this is, and I would beat the breaks off of her. So, what I did was, I sent Linda to go sit by Abby and talk to her so I could go see what's going on with my son. When I went to go talk to him, he was standing in the dining room talking to his father, so I let it go.

As I stood in the kitchen watching my husband and my son in one room, I could still see Linda and Abby talking in the other room. I acted like I was wiping the counter down so no one would notice that I was trying to put two and two together. When it was all over, everyone met back up in the living room and we all chatted for a minute then DJ said they were about to go. We all said our goodbyes and DJ and Abby left first. Linda got her things and said she was going back to the hotel so she could pack and get ready to leave tomorrow. But she hesitated until DJ and Abby left. She claimed she misplaced her keys and wanted me to help look for them. Me being the type of person that I am, I knew that isn't what she was doing because the woman took an Uber to get here. So, I said I would look for them with her. Dylan went upstairs to get ready for bed and DJ and Abby left. My son gave me a hug and kissed me on my forehead and said see you tomorrow, then they left.

After the coast was clear, Linda and I sat down at the table so we could talk. "Auntie, your girl is a little off." I looked at Linda and said, "What do you mean?" She said, "When I was talking to her, all she talked about was DJ this and DJ that. When I asked her questions about herself, all she did was answered them with questions about DJ and me." "DJ and you?" I said. "Yeah, she asked me how were we cousins, who was related to whom that made us cousins, how long have we been close cousins, was I the only female cousin he had and if there were any more female cousins. And if so, where do they live, and do they come around him as much as I do? Ole girl was about to get cussed out! But I kept my composer and I answered as little as possible. Where did he get psycho Betty from, the mental hospital? Maybe she just really wanted to know because he talked about being her husband one day."

As I listened to Linda talk, I knew then, what I was feeling was real. "Auntie?" Linda said, I think you need to watch her. Don't tell DJ how you are feeling just yet, just see how things go for a while, invite her over more so you can see how DJ is, then make your conclusion. He seems happy, so let him be happy, he is grown, and he must learn certain things on his own. Just like you use to tell DJ and I when we were little, "Watch and Pray". You are a smart woman Auntie; you'll know when something changes. I must go now, my uber driver just pulled up. I will be back in two weeks. I'm taking my vacation and I was going to go to Florida for my vacation, but I think I want to spend my two weeks here if you don't mind."

I told her "Sure, that would be great Lin, we would love to have you here. It would give me something to do while Dylan is working."

So, as she left, I closed and locked all the doors and went upstairs with Dylan. When I got upstairs, he was already stretched out across the bed watching the news. I walked in and asked him was everything okay, he said yes and that I should get ready for bed. I went into the restroom to take a shower and get ready for bed then my phone made a noise. I picked up my phone and it was DJ texting. He sent me a text saying good night and he enjoyed dinner and he would see us tomorrow. I texted goodnight back and that we loved him.

As I got into the bed, I asked my husband what him and DJ talk about today. All he said was, "Guy stuff." I don't know why, but when Dylan says that, it turns my gears. So, mommas can't know about guy stuff? Gee-whiz! Anyway, as time went on, we noticed how we began to see less and less of DJ. It started off with him missing Sunday dinners, then the nightly check ins he did with me and his dad to let us know he was home and safe. It's not like we were keeping tabs on him, but with everything going on in this world, DJ just wanted to let us know he was ok. It was his idea for the nightly check ins. We did the same for him, we texted him when we were headed to bed and if he didn't get a text from us, he would call to see if we were ok. My husband always said, when everyone leaves out of your life, your family should always be there for you no matter what. Of course, a lot of families aren't like that anymore, but still, your parents' home should always be open to their children. No matter what.

Time went on and then red flag number two was shown. DJ came to his father and asked to borrow some money. That has never happened. DJ works with his dad and his dad pays him well, why would he be asking for money? Once again, my husband said stay out of it and leave it up to him and DJ. I listened to my husband and stayed out of it. DJ was healthy and still looked like my son, so I knew it wasn't drugs or anything.

The week came when it was time for Linda to come a visit for two weeks and I couldn't be more overjoyed about he arrival. Dylan sister and I were really close before she passed away and our children were like brother and sister almost. Linda was three years older than DJ so they kind of grew up together almost. By the time Linda flew back in from New York, I hadn't seen DJ in a week. We talked everyday but he didn't come to the house. My husband saw him every day but for some reason, DJ always made excuses not to come see his mother.

When Linda came, we spent a few hours talking and catching up on things and how NY life was treating her. Then she brought up DJ. I told her everything and how I felt about certain things and she informed me that she would do her part to find out if he was ok and that he was safe. And that's exactly what she did.

The next day of her being back in Memphis, Lin texted DJ to see if he was available for lunch to hang out for a while and he agreed. They were going to Lin's favorite restaurant in downtown Memphis and they were going to meet up there. Later that night, Lin came back to the house and things seemed to be ok, so I didn't worry. She told me that her and DJ were going to go hang out again the next day and I was totally fine with that. As she settled in, she came downstairs to my office and sat next to my desk where I was working.

"Auntie, I know what's going on with DJ." When she said that, I dropped everything I was doing, and I was ready to listen with an open mind.

"Auntie, Abby is a control freak. She wants DJ to herself and don't want to share him with anyone that is a female, not even you. The reason why he hasn't been around is because she always gives him a reason why he can't leave her right then. If it's not her head hurting, it's him giving her time and attention. If it's not that, then she'll say that she made plans for them to do something together. If a woman does come around him, she will make a big deal about it. That's why she asked me so many questions about who I was, how were we related, and how close we were as a family. She's obsessed with him and very jealous hearted. She believes that he shouldn't be around any other women but her, that's why he spends more time with Uncle Dylan than he does with you and you're his mother. She thinks that he is seeing another woman or the neighbor's daughter and you will cover for him. The girl is psychotic and deranged if you ask me. Of course, if you tell him this, he will think you just don't like her, and you are trying to keep them apart, so he won't listen to you. He will have to see it for himself, no matter how many times we can warn him. Truthfully, we need to catch it before it's too late."

"After Lin told me that, I was appalled. We sat and talked a while longer while I tried to come up with a reason to get him over here without her coming with him. I thought to myself, maybe what Lin said was just her opinion of the matter. Maybe she was saying it because she didn't like the fact that Abby was asking her all these questions. All I know is that my son was not acting like the man we know and love."

I looked up from my notes and began to ask Treasure some questions. "Mrs. Treasure? I would like to ask you a few questions if you don't mind. What does an obsession over your son have anything to do with you calling this woman the devil? Did she harm him in any way? Did she take him completely way from you? And most of all, where is DJ now?" After asking those questions, I noticed that she had become aggravated about what I said.

"Mrs. Kris, right now my son is at Garvin's Institute and Behavioral Health Center, an hour away from here. He has been there for about three weeks now. He will be released next week." As I sat there in disbelief, all I could do is offer my sympathy. "Mrs. T, why is he there?"

Well about a month ago, we noticed that he wasn't eating enough, he had started to miss work more and more every week. When we called his cell phone, she would always answer it and give us every excuse in the book on way he couldn't come to the phone. The last time he came over, she sat in the car until he came back out, she texted him the whole time he was in the house visiting his father and me. Unfortunately, that was the time when I had a church group over here and it was all women in our home. When she saw all the women leaving out of the house, the texts started to come back to back to the point that we couldn't have a conversation with him without him stopping to answer her text. So, I asked him to go outside and tell her to come in the house if she wanted to know what was going on in my home. He put the phone down and went out to the car to get her and bring her in the house, then we were able to have a conversation with our son.

When he went outside, I peeped out the window to see if she would come in and I saw her yelling at my son. I couldn't hear everything she was saying to him, but I knew she was saying something he didn't like. While she was walking up to the house, Sister Irene was walking past them, and she spoke to DJ and Abby. DJ looked down at his feet and continued to walk while Abby looked Sister Irene dead in her face and said, "Hello, thank you for stopping by." Sister Irene turned to her and said, "This isn't your house." then she continued to walk away.

That night, Sister Irene called me, and this is what she said. "Mrs. T, sorry to call you so late, I know it's 9:30 at night but something has been weighing heavily on my spirit since I left your house. Do you mind me asking, who that young lady was that was walking with DJ earlier as I was leaving our prayer group?" I held the phone in my hand for a second because when Sister Irene says something is weighing on her spirit, it usually isn't good news. After a ten second pause, I said, "Oh, yes, her name is Abby, that is my son's girlfriend. They've been dating for almost a year now."

I heard Sister Irene take a deep breath and she said, "Well Sister, he needs to get far away from her. That young lady's spirit ain't right. When I walked outside and they were still standing by the car, I heard her tell him, "You really want me to kill myself don't you? All those women coming out of your parents' home! Which one of them was for you? I told you, if anything happens to our relationship, I will kill myself, I love you so much. No one can have you but me and me only. I love you more than God and your parents love you. Don't you know that sweetie?" then she gave him a kiss.

When I finally reached eye to eye contact with them, I said, "Hello to them both, and all he did was look down and she said, "Thanks for stopping by." that's when I said what I said to her. Treasure? That girl is felled with some demon's honey. We strongly need to pray for a release from her. Has he ever acted like that before?"

I held on to the phone very tightly because I didn't know if I wanted to breakdown in tears or go after that female for what she is doing to my son. If your child is grown and making his own life decisions, how do you address this without getting into your child's life? How do you try to stop it while the whole time she is calling your son a mamma's boy because he wants to listen to his mother on certain things? Do you let it go and let him learn from his mistakes, do you speak to your child and let the chips fall where they may, or do you fight for your child because he is in a dangerous relationship? What is a parent to do? Two months ago, DJ changed his diet because she changed hers. That's why he stopped coming to Sunday dinners, because she didn't like what Dylan and I fix for dinner. Then, he stopped working with his father because she told him all they talk about was women in a sexual nature and that all the men he works with want to sleep with her. Then, she deleted Linda's number out of his phone so they couldn't keep in touch and got a family plan phone in his name so she could keep up with his location at all times when he leaves the house, she'll be able to track his every move. On top of that, they moved in together four months ago and she installed cameras inside and outside the house to watch everything when she's gone with her family and hanging out with her brother Collin and his friends. She said she did that so she can feel safe when DJ isn't home.

A few nights ago, my husband and I were talking, and I asked my him what he thought about all of this. He told me, "the devil comes in all shapes and forms. No matter how many times we can talk to our love ones, they still will make their own choices in life. In this matter right here, Jr is going to have to ask God for help with this one, it's out of our hands. Sometimes God will allow us to go through the storms, but it's up to us to decided rather we keep going or do we stop and wait until the storm is over. Most people would stop and wait it out, but the smart ones would keep going until they see blue skies. That's what we need to do Treasure, let Jr go through this storm himself, God got him, all we need to do is be waiting for our son on the other side of the rainbow to comfort him when he returns."

When my husband said that, all I wanted him to do was go to sleep or go to his man cave and leave me alone. Yes, what my husband said was true, but at the same time, I wanted to fix it myself, I wanted to find that female and tell her how I really feel about her and this whole thing and maybe lay these hands on her too! It's my son! My only child! and the devil has him right where she wants him. How can I be calm?! My son is in a mental institute because of her! She has ruined what Dylan and I took 27 years to build! How am I supposed to feel? What did I do to God for this to come back on my son?! I never say I hate anyone, but this female right here, I hate with a passion! Why? Because she knew what she was doing! She knew it!

After Mrs. T. took a deep breath, "She pulled my son away from all his friends, made him change jobs, stopped him from coming to Sunday dinner, pulled him away from the church, and just locked him in a closet, away from everyone. She used sex and suicided to keep my son right where she wants him. Mrs. Kris, I know what you're thinking, how can I blame all of this on her? He has a part in it as well. Your right, it's a 50/50 deal in a relationship. He could have walked away at any time; but he chose to stay together because he thought he was showing love to a person he cared so deeply about. I know now, that's why he put up with it and why he changed for her, he was doing it out of love.

See when we raise our children, we tell them the good and the bad areas in life. How to be a responsible adult, how to money manage, how to pay bills. We let them know that education is important and how to take care of difficult situations. We teach them about how to be respectful to their elders, (not everyone teaches that to their kids) we teach them about religion, and just how to be a good person all around. But how many times do we teach them how to look out for bad people? How to notice if the people we hanging out with has good intentions and how to look for the real love? We don't teach our children and teenagers the rights and wrongs of a toxic relationship. We teach all about love, love, love, never about a toxic relationship because we trust our kids enough to tell the different. But what if we meet a person who had a rough life growing up? Do we treat them any different? No, we don't. We supposed to show love to those as well and that's what my son did, but with this particular person, it drove him crazy."

As I looked at Mrs. T, I saw hurt, sadness, and joy in her eyes. So, I asked my last two questions. "Mrs. Treasure, what led up to your son's breakdown and are they still together?"

When I said that, relief and joy came over her face. I didn't know what she was about to say so I prepared myself. I double checked my tape recorder, I pulled out more paper for my notes and I sat quietly until she was ready.

"When it all boiled down, I decided to call for backup. See what most people don't know is, I have street soldiers that will go to battle for me if I make one phone call. That one phone call can shut this entire community down if they choose too. This click will stand together and fight any and everything that stands in their way, and all I had to do is make a phone call. So, I did, I had no other choice. My husband said let the storm ride out and it will all be over. But sometimes in life, if you see someone in a storm, and you notice that they are trying to get out of it but can't seem to find their way. You must go into their storm and help them out. Help them to see that people are there to help and to guide them on their way. At times, people will have baggage with them, and they try to bring that baggage with them through the storm and it doesn't work like that. That baggage is what's keeping you from walking out of your storm because it's too heavy to carry. Leave it there. We don't pull you out of your own storm, we guide you, you must walk out yourself, alone, with the help of Jesus Christ.

One day, three weeks ago, I waited until my husband went to work. I grabbed my bible and prayed to God to help my son in the mist of his storm. Show him how to recognize that he is in a toxic relationship. I asked Him to bless Abby, to heal whatever was broken inside her that needs to be fixed. Whatever is going on in her life, it had to have been taught to her, she had to have had some things happen to her to even act like this with men. Bless her Heavenly Father. After I said my prayers, I picked up the phone and made that phone call.

"Hello, I need you more than ever. How fast can you get here? We need to speak before my husband gets home, it's time that all of this comes to an end. I'll be waiting." Then I hung up. Within 30 minutes after making that phone call, it was a knock at my door. My heart raced, my palms got sweaty, my throat was dry, and my spirit felt weak. When I finally opened the door, I only heard two words, "You ready?"

Sister Irene and all 15 of my prayer warrior sisters were standing at my doorstep strapped tight with the word of God in one hand, prayer cloths, and anointing oils in the other hand. It was the most beautiful army of Angels I have ever seen in my life. The spirit of the Lord was on all over these women. I felt the presents of God on ever soul that was standing in front of me. I know the presents of the Lord when I feel it, and it was definitely there.

They all marched in one by one with the strength of a lion and the power of Christ Jesus in their hearts. As we all sat down, the room got quiet and Sister Irene began to speak.

"Ladies, we are all here to help our dear sister Mrs. Treasure Possession and her son Dylan Jr. We all have heard the stories, seen the difference in him, even my husband said how different DJ was on the job. My husband has been working with Dylan Sr. for 11 years and never once has he seen DJ withdrawn like he was. We must pray for him and the young lady that he is with. We will ask the Lord for guidance, protection, healing, and knowledge on how to rid this evil spirit from these blind individuals. We are here for you Treasure, we will stand by you no matter what, in Jesus Holy Name!"

"As I sat there watching my sisters pray in silence, I glanced at the room we all were in and I couldn't do anything but thank the Lord God for such beautiful women in my life. I closed my eyes and began to pray. When we were all done, Sister Thelma asked me what happened and what is it that we all need to do. Sister Irene took a chair from the dining room and sat it in the middle of the floor so everyone could hear me. Then I began to talk. I told them what has been happening to my son and Abby's relationship and how it affected his mental wellbeing, how my son stopped coming over, how he quit his job working with his dad that he was doing since he was thirteen, how he lost so much weight because he changed his diet for her and how he is now in a mental facility due to depression and him having a breakdown in the middle of the grocery store which led him to be admitted in to the hospital. The more I described what's going on, the more I noticed that the women were getting mad. Then one of our sisters spoke. Sister Lilly S. looked up from her bible and said, "Treasure, about three weeks or so, I ran into your son in the parking lot of the grocery store. He must have been with Abby; I didn't know it was her because she was stand offish while I was talking to him. Now I know who that was that was giving me an evil look. I just thought we were blocking her car or something. Before he could introduce me to her, I looked at her and said, "Hey, I know you, your dating my brother's son, Collin! How are you? Are we in your way?" and before I could say anything else, she said, "You are now." Then she got into the car. I had no idea all of that was connected. I wondered why DJ stood there like he seen a ghost. I gave him a huge hug and said tell your mom I said Hi, then I walked away. I had no idea they were together. I'm so sorry Treasure, please forgive me for not saying anything."

I looked at Sister Lilly and said, "It's okay my sister, God has a way of revealing things to us in perfect timing. It's funny though, three weeks ago, my son was admitted into Garvin's Hospital just around the time of your encounter. Could that have been his breaking point?"

The other sisters shook their heads in agreement and was amazed how God started to work on our behalf so fast. As we sat there and prayed for my son, Abby, and my husband, I knew then God was working for our good. His word says in Matthew 18:20**, (NIV)**

20 "For where two or three gather in my name, there am I with them."

God knows what He is doing all the time. We said a special prayer for my husband because no matter how hard he tries to hide it; he misses his son deeply. He claims he is trying to let a man be a man, but men need Gods help too.

The more we prayed the more things came out, it's amazing how small the world is. While we were praying, Sister Jasmine asked a question that shocked me to my bones. "Sister Treasure, is Abby's real name Abigail Tucker? If so, I know her father, Charles Tucker.

You all have been talking about Abby this and Abby that, but I never knew her as Abby, always Abigail. I was her nanny when she was four years old. I only worked for them for about a year or so, very short-term job for me. He was married to another lady when Abigail was born, it was a scandalous affair. He was beating on his wife while spoiling the other woman. Abigail was born out of an adulterous relationship and he was her father. He mentally abused Abigail all the time. He kept her mother away from her as much as possible, he wanted her mother all to himself and that's how I got the job being her nanny. He never spent time with her, he never showed her attention and when her mom used to go out with friends or family, he would always say he'll die without her. So, she stayed home all the time and that's how I ended up living with them for six months. I couldn't handle it anymore, so I called Child Protective Services and reported what I witnessed and then I left. Her mom left with Abigail and moved away years ago, but recently moved back about a year ago. Dear God! What is this? It all makes since now!"

"All the women in the room started shouting and praising God, Women was kneeling in His presents, some were speaking in tongues, and others just started crying screaming thank you God! Mrs. Kris, what I experienced in that room was the presents of Jesus Christ and only He can make the blind see, the weak strong and the dead wake up again. I love the Lord, and I will thank Him every day for the rest of my life."

As I sat there listening to the amazing story this woman of God just told me, I couldn't do anything but praise God with her. It was mind blowing how deeper things were coming out in the mist of it all. I was speechless.

"Once we all came together, we prayed for the healing of those two souls, Abby and DJ. The Lord works in mysterious ways, and no matter how hard it gets, always look towards Him for healing. Teach our children the good and the bad in life so they will know its ok to mess up sometimes, but it's not ok to stay in our mess."

When she said those things, I thought about my own life, my husband, my kids, and my future. How I procrastinated on my writing and how I need to get closer to God in my life. After about 15 minutes, we heard car doors close. The doorbell rang and Treasure went to open the door. It was about 10 or 12 women standing at the door. They all came in smiling and laughing while hugging each other and fellowshipping with one another. It was a beautiful site to see woman of all ages and race fellowshipping together. The ladies brought food and snacks for everyone. While the ladies were getting things together, I introduced myself to everyone, I seen Sister Irene pulled Treasure to the side. When I glanced over at them, Treasure made a gesture for me to come over to them.

"Mrs. Kris, Treasure said, may I introduce to you Sister Irene, my sister in Christ and my sister for life. She is my real sister. Her and I have the same dad, she's just older than me by 50 years." They both laughed and then Sis. Irene thumbed Treasure on the forehead. "Mrs. Kris, Sis. Irene said, I really admire what you are doing and how you will reach a lot of people when your done with your book. But the best is yet to come."

As she said that, Treasure had a strange look on her face, "What does that mean might I ask? Are you going to try and be in her book too?" Before Sis. Irene could say something, we heard another person say, "The best is already here." Then everyone got quiet. When I turned around, I saw two handsome men standing in the doorway. The looked almost identical to each other, it was breath taking. Before we knew it, Treasure ran right past everyone and grabbed the youngest one and started crying and screaming out to Jesus yelling, "Thank you God!" we then heard the young man say, "God let me hear your prayers momma, and I'm home. I'm so sorry momma." Then he broke down in tears.

The women in the room praised God so loud that you couldn't hear anything else in the room but heaven rejoicing with them. I looked over at the two and I broke down in tears. How could a person not feel the love of God in this room? We all started thanking God and praising Him at the same time. In the mist of me praying, Sister Irene walked over to me and gave me a huge hug. She whispered in my ear, "Dylan Sr. called us and told us he was bringing Jr home today and Jr should meet everyone who helped him see his way through the storm. So, I did." I looked at her and said, "This was amazing, just to be a part of this reunion is priceless. Thank You." She gave me another hug then walked over there to congratulate her sister. As they all enjoyed each other's company. I slowly grabbed my things and headed towards the side door in the kitchen. Before I left, I wrote Treasure a note that read,

"The time I spent with you will be a moment I will never forget. You've shown me how far the love of a mother would go for her child no matter how old they are and what road they take in life. It was a pleasure, and an honor to go on this journey with you, I pray to see you all again soon. Thank you from the bottom of my heart. You are truly, a "Daughter of God"

- **Mrs. Kris**

WHEN I MADE IT TO MY CAR, SOMEONE CALLED OUT MY NAME. It startled me for a minute then I realized it was DJ calling out to me. As I turned around, he walked closer to me and reached out his hand to shake it. "Mrs. Kris, I really appreciate what you did for my mother. Thank you for letting her be your book. Now we can have something to look back on in the future to see what God can bring anyone through. Thank you again."

I smiled at him and said, "She helped me just by listening to her story, I thought about my own family as well. But I do have a question. What happened to Abby? Did you all break up or is she still around?" He smiled and said,

"Yeah, we broke up when I found out she was seeing someone else while we were together. Then a few people came to see her and talked to her off and on while I was away, so she wrote me a letter apologizing for all the things she put me through. Then she moved out of Memphis to go stay with her Aunt in Wisconsin. It ended on bittersweet terms, but it is, what it is. May God get the glory. Well, I'll see you at the book signing once you finish, I know my mom can't wait until you're done. May God be with you Mrs. Kris."

He reached and gave me a huge hug and ran back to the house. I smiled as I walked away thinking how awesome God is. When I got in the car, I put on my seat belt then glanced one more time at the house. That's when I saw Treasure waving at me out the window saying goodbye with the note, in her hands. Joy filled the air and God shined down on their home. I waved back at her with tears of joy in my eyes, I whispered, Thank You to her and drove away.

Her name is Treasure Possession, and she and all 15 of her soldiers for Christ, are "The Daughters of God."

CHAPTER 5
WISDOM RAIN

"I don't know anything about God, I never met Him. As far as I know, he is just as real as the tooth fairy. Just like those parents that tell their children about Santa Clause, the Easter bunny, and the stork that brings babies to expecting parents who wanted to have children. Could Jesus be a myth just like those stories? Think about it, we never seen him, we never met him, and we never touched him. But people still talk to them all the time. How far can a story go? Well, apparently, this story goes back to the beginning of time. How is it that in the beginning of the bible, it describes how the world was made, it's funny because who was around when that happened, so how in the world did they know how God created the world? Who wrote that?

It was said that the bible is the greatest book ever written, so if that is true, why is it that when you google the greatest books ever written, the bible is nowhere on the list? Really? Come on people, I do believe that the bible was written by people who seen things and experienced things in the old days, that part I do not deny, but, out of all the things Jesus supposed to have done, that's all you come up with? His birth, and when he was thirty years old, is all we got from that book. Did he do miracles when he was a toddler, did he do miracles when he was a teenager? And what happened to Joseph after he was born? Did Mary and Joseph split up after the birth? Think about it, an angel appears to Mary and tells her she is going to get pregnant, she goes and tells Joseph that she is pregnant by God. Joseph already had his own thoughts in his head that's why he left until an angel appeared to him and told him to go back. Then he stayed with her until Christ was born and then we don't here nothing else from Joseph in the bible. Why? He knew that baby wasn't his and so he stayed with her till she delivered and then he leaves because deep down he knew that baby wasn't his and did he really believe Mary when she told him that she was pregnant by God.

Those are the questions people like me ask. Those are the questions that people like me get viewed as an atheist or a devil worshipping person. The church gets upset when we ask questions like that, they get frustrated, they get offended, or they will get defensive because people like me ask too many questions. The last time I asked a pastor some of those questions, do you know what he told me? He looked me dead in my eyes and said, "I don't know, you have to research it for yourself. You must seek God yourself and he will reveal himself to you." Then he invited me to come to his church for services and attend bible study classes. Never once could he answer my questions. So, if the people in the world like me have those type of questions, then who do we go to for the answer? The Bible, The Pastor, or God?

My family are very holy people, they raised me up in the church until I was old enough to tell them that I didn't want to attend anymore. I wanted to search for this God myself. So, I enrolled into a seminary college just to search for this God that everyone seems to want to worship. I wanted to know who this God was and why everyone called on His son Jesus the Christ, or is it Jesus Christ? Anyway, the best way I could find out is go looking for myself.

When I was 15 years old, my best friend died from a very rear disease. Her family grieved for months after she passed away. They prayed to God for healing, comfort, and for answers. All they got was pure silence. No one came to answer their questions, no Pastor could explain why God allowed this to happen, and no comfort came to them after Bella's death. Mrs. Kris, do you know what happened then? People just kept bringing food to the house, people kept saying that they are going to pray for them, or they will have them in their prayers. But do these so-called Christians actually pray for these people, or is it something they all say just to make themselves feel better? We all know not everyone really prays for people when they say they do. If they really prayed for these people, then my best friend Bella wouldn't have died! You hear pastor's say all the time, "Where two or three gather in my name, there am I with them." That's what the bible says in Matthew 18:20. So, if this is true, why in the hell did my best friend die? Why even let Bella come into this world if He was going to take her right back out! Why?! What is the purpose for all of this? That was unnecessary heartache for her family and for me! Why would God bless families with children then take them right back from them! Totally unnecessary! I knew then at the age of 15, that I had to find God and ask Him myself."

As I sat there in her office at her home, I realized that Wisdom is very heartbroken. I realized that people can go through life carrying something inside them so deep that it will affect the rest of their lives. The littlest things can change a person's life as they know it. Rather it be traumatic or just saying words to a person without you knowing that it hurts them, can turn someone's world upside down.

Wisdom continued, "Words can heal, kill, and it can tattoo itself into someone's mind. Many wars happened from saying the wrong words. Many people in the world have died because someone said the wrong words to another person. My dad always told me that you can kill someone physically and mentally with just words. He said words are just words, but they carry so much power. He said that the bible stated that, "life and death are in the power of the tongue and those who love it will eat of it's fruit. (Proverb 18:21). Out of all the things I have researched about the bible, that one scripture always stood out to me. You may ask me why, well because I have seen it many of times. But, if life and death are in the power of the tongue, then why did prayers kill my best friend at 15?" Here I am forty-five years old and I still hold on to her death. What does that say about me?"

Has my life been affected by this to the point I had to search for God myself? I would say so. I spent many, many years in college searching for God. I took a sabbatical from my job a few years ago to go on a spiritual retreat to Israel. It was the most amazing thing I had ever experienced in my life. The culture, the fellowship, the dedication that those people had towards the Lord changed my life. Mrs. Kris, if you ever get a chance to travel to Israel, please go, it is a life changing experience that I believe every person who is searching for God should go. It is pricey though. You will have to save money just for the plane ticket. It was around $4,000 to go for a week, but it was worth every penny. I was able to venture to the place that Jesus was born, I was able to visit the place that John the Baptist visited, and to the Holy Sepulcher and stand in the place that Jesus tomb was reported to be. But the most amazing thing about my trip was The Western Wall, the Wailing Wall in Jerusalem. Before I decided to approach the wall, I sat back for awhile just to see and be in aww of what I was seeing. The men were in one area and the woman had to be in the other area of the wall. You had a choice to go to the wall and pray or you could write your prayers down and place them in the wall inside the cracks.

As I sat there just looking out on the people and seeing how dedicated everyone was praying at this wall, I decided to do what I always wanted to do. To ask God why was He silent in my life, why did He take Bella from me, why did He allow me to go through my teenage years as an outcast that was bullied in school before Bella died, and is He really real?

I felt that if the Lord wouldn't answer me, then I will just go to the place where he walked and talked and ask Him myself. Isn't that what most people do? If they have an issue with someone and is very important that they need to talk about it, then why not meet up at the place where you know where he would be at the most. The Holy Land. Every pain I had in my heart, every question that I had in my soul and in my spirit, I brought with me. As I look upon the people that were crying and praying, all I could do was cry myself. As I stood there looking at the people, I found myself walking closer and closer to the wall. The more I got closer to the wall, the more I started to feel a sensation over me of hurt, pain, sadness, and comfort at the same time. How can you feel peace and comfort while in total turmoil? I guess that is what my dad always talked about, how God can calm the storm in the mist of fire and rage in one's heart.

Once I made it to the wall, I heard prayers in many different languages, they cried out to the Lord for the hurt, for the deaths, for the chaos that life experiences had emptied into their lives. As I got closer to the wall, I saw an elderly woman on her knees crying out to the Lord saying, "Thank You Jesus, Thank You Lord! You are the All mighty and wonderful God! Praise be Your Name!"

I looked at her strangely as I continued towards the wall. For some reason, I thought of the time when my father and mother sat me down in the living room on my 13ᵗʰ birthday and they told me a story about why my name is Wisdom Rain. My dad started off with a scripture from the New King James Version of the bible, (2 Chronicles 1:11-12), were God offered Solomon anything his heart desired. All Solomon said was, "Wisdom". My father said that is what he asked God for, when I was born, he asked me to grow up with wisdom and knowledge of his word. He told me that God answered his prayers that day. I asked him how he knew God answered his prayers and he said, "Because it rained right after I asked Him to give you wisdom when you were born." I asked my father was that a good thing that it rained when he asked God for wisdom for me and he told me,

"Baby girl, God will answer you in ways that you, that person could understand. God doesn't answer everyone in the same way. He answers people in ways that only they would understand. My answer from God won't be the same as the answer God will give your mother. We can ask the same question to God, and he will give us our answers in totally different ways, only we, the individual, would understand. I had a friend whose daughter was born on a rainy day as well, his name was Theos, it was joyous and sad occasion. His wife died giving birth to their daughter. They had a tree fall through the window while it was raining, and they didn't know that the tree had pierced her side during childbirth. He named his daughter Storm, he is a blessed man, and I know everything happens for a reason and the reason will only be revealed to those who choose to see the works of God. No matter how things turn out, it's a reason behind everything. So, that's how I got my name, Dr. Wisdom Rain Charleston, PhD.

I finally approached the wall, as I stood there gazing at this huge stone wall, I saw little pieces of papers sticking out from every direction. I saw women with handkerchiefs and prayer clothes, women with all types of bibles and prayer books in their hands. It was unbelievable, it didn't matter what race you were, it didn't matter, what language you spoke, what you believe or didn't believe, they were all there for the same reason, God.

Before I could begin to pray, the woman that was just crying out to the Lord approached me and said, "This is going to change your life, no matter what you going through, pray about it, ask for wisdom, place it on the wall and let God do the rest. I praised God because I just lost my husband last month and I needed closer. I was running myself insane because he was all I had. We had no children and only a few friends. We were too busy to enjoy life and it killed him with a massive heart attack. Now I'm alone."

She looked so sad; it really broke my heart. If she can come all the way to Jerusalem to ask for healing from the Lord. How could a person trust the Lord so much that she flew thousands of miles to ask for healing? Where was my trust in God through all of this? I spent my entire life searching for God and He was with me they hold time.

I put my frustrations to the side, I put my doubt to the side, I put all my fears and questions to the side, and I did something my father told me to do years ago, I submitted to God. I put my hands on the wall and instantly, I started crying. I gave myself to Him, my search for God was finally over, I knew He was in the mist of my prayers and I felt His love all over my body. I felt a small breeze brush across my face that had the sweetest smell. Suddenly, I fell to my knees and yelling out Glory! I prayed for healing, I prayed for comfort, I pray for Bella, and I prayed for something I never prayed for before, wisdom.

Knowing that I was standing in a place that the Lord came to pray and teach was mind-blowing. The history, the dedication, and the faith that people have there is unbelievable. I gave myself to the Lord and I never looked back. I asked God for forgiveness for all the things I said, the things that I showed doubt for. I searched for Him all my life and the whole time; he was preparing me for this journey. The whole time, He was there. He watched me search for Him, He heard my cries, He guided me in the path to meet Him there to the Western Wall and placed you Mrs. Kris in my path to get to me. Yes, I hated God so much that I spent my entire life looking for Him and all I had to do was ask to see Him and He came right when I needed Him the most. Praise be to God!

I did this interview with you because I know for a fact that there are men and women out there that hate God for a lot of reasons, I was one of them. He was there for me every step of the way. Soon as I touched the wall, every question that I had since I was 13 came flooding back to me. But this time, God provided the answers to me and it felt like I was taking trip back in time. He showed me Bella praying to Him to take her away because she was tired of her and her family suffering with her condition. He showed me my parents crying because I stopped following Him. He showed me the time I ran outside in the rain and yelled out, "Where are You!? while in the mist of my rage because people left, and right were getting hurt and bad things were happening to my family that I couldn't explain. He showed me everything, and all I did was touch the wall with my fingertips.

I spent the rest of my trip visiting different sites and holy places to get as much of the Lord experience as I could. I visited the Dead Sea; I visit Bethlehem and just took my time and walked the streets of the cities I visited. Being able to be in the same place Christ was in is a feeling only a person who has been there could experience. Mrs. Kris, if you ever get a chance to go, be sure to take your husband, or even make it a trip with the church, I know they would love it.

No matter what goes on in your life, no matter how hard things can and will get in this world, the Lord will never leave you nor forsake you. I'm talking to the person reading this book that feels like life is hard and it seems to be no way out, no signs of relief. I'm talking to that person that feels that God isn't real, but something brought you out of what you went through. I'm talking to that person that is struggling with a secret that could change someone's life if it was revealed. Remember, God see's everything.

I'm talking to the drug addict that seems to just can't get away from that situation, the child that is afraid to tell their parents that they are pregnant or expecting a child. That married person that has committed adultery and to ashamed to confess. I'm talking to that person who sleeps around and never wanted to settle down because you are so use to people taking care of you.

God will deliver you from everything if you only submit to Him and let Him take hold of your life so He can guide you to His Kingdom. At the end of the day, no matter what your going through, He is there, standing next to you just waiting on you to ask for help. The Lord said in Matthew 7:7, "Ask and it will be given to you; seek and you will find; knock and the door will be open to you." So many people forget about that scripture, they only call on Him when it's too late or down to the wire. Why?

We need to talk to Him every day, as much time we spend on social media, working, watching television, and having our hands full with cell phones clicking likes on everything that is posted, how much time do we take out of our day just to say thank you? How many times a day do we open our bible and just read a chapter or a paragraph a day? How many times has a person opened a bible or even used a bible to read or teach? What happened to people bringing real bibles to church? Now it's tablets and cell phones. Don't teach anyone from a tablet, or your cell phone, this is a church, a Holy place. People need to use the bible and read from the pages that God has blessed! You use the same electronic device that you look up sinful things on, you made unholy phone calls with, and yet, you use this same device to come preach with! That's just plain wrong! But, that's just my opinion of the matter. I feel comfortable in saying all of that because I lived it already and I've seen it at plenty of churches.

I was a person who hated God so much that I made it my life's mission to prove he didn't exist. I respect everyone's beliefs, that doesn't mean my beliefs are better than theirs and theirs are better than mine. At the end of the day, we all must believe in something beyond this world. It's up to you to search for the truth, it might not be what you expected to be, but at least you searched and found the answers to the questions we all had, and that's, "Lord, where are you?"

When you ask God a question, you will get an answer. We all just need to learn to see and hear them when He does. Watch and pray, listen in the mist silence, and open your eyes when He is right next to you. When the Lord is around you, you will feel his presence all through your body. Embrace it, love it, and take hold of it and never let it go, no matter what, because He will never let you go.

My name is Wisdom Rain, and I am, The Daughter of God.

CHAPTER 6
HEAVEN GATES

The day I met Heaven; I knew I wanted to hear her story. It was something about her that made me want to get to know her more. She had an uplifting spirit about her, and I knew then we were going to be great friends.

I came to her home one Saturday afternoon just so we can go have lunch together, when I noticed she wasn't herself that day. That's when I knew, she had somethings to get off her chest, so, I cancelled our lunch date and we sat and talked, sometimes friends just need that person to listen without being judged or criticized. So., I listened. This is what she told me..

"I became saved at the age of 15, and when I became saved, I became saved through how the Lord used my mom. I've always been in a very religious family and my mom and my family has always been my support system and as I grew up in a church home that was in Mississippi.

One day the church we attended performed a play called "Judgement Day" and I had always wondered about God. Going to church, I had many questions, but I didn't know a whole lot, but I was always that kind of person that always wanted to learn more. When I would hear sermons preached, I use to wonder about this so-called Higher Power (as people as people put it), I had to learn that this was God. I used to wonder who wakes us up in the morning, who gives us our health and our strength to be able to get around every day or make it through whatever we go through. So, as they did this play called judgement day, it was one of our ministers play and they had choir members as the people that was God's children that was the ones being judged. Each member had a certain song that they had to sing which was expressing their life stories and my mother had so sing "Amazing Grace" one of my favorite songs to this day. They all walked in with white robes so they can receive their gold crowns from the Lord. I watched them all walk down the aisle dressed in all white and I glanced over and that's when I stood up and saw my mother, I could see the spirit of God on her and in her as she entered the sanctuary. Destiny, my mother, walked in and began singing Amazing Grace and right then, when she sang the verse "a wrench like me" that's when the spirit of Christ hit me right then. At age 15, I had made up in my mind this is what I wanted in my life. I made the decision at a young age of 15 to give my all to the Lord. Even though I was still learning about Christ, I got the opportunity to work with the youths at church teaching Sunday School and help them understand more about Christ and I really enjoyed doing that. I was still a babe in Christ, and I was still learning but I wanted to know more, and I wanted to do more.

It's funny because when I mention it to my mom now, she doesn't even remember that day. It was something in me that thrived to love and find out more about God. I had to search for Him myself, I had to find Him and learn to call out to Him with my spirit, all at the age of 15 years old. Therefore, I am telling my story because I hope that my life and experiences that I been through and that God has brought me out of can be a blessing to for somebody else. I want my life to be testimony that would help somebody else.

My name is Heaven Gates, and this is my story.

For me, around that age 15, children tend to act like they from another planet between the ages of 15 and 19 years old. But for me that was a challenging time for me. I was going to Cornerstone High School in Delaware at the time and doing that year, I was going through lots of challenges. It was like I was still trying to find myself; I didn't belong anywhere; I didn't fit in with the end crowd or anything. It's funny because I was the oldest out of eight kids, I still felt like I was by myself, I didn't have anybody I could call on or talk too or to just be there for me at that time.

Doing that year, I found myself going through things all alone, I felt lonely. I didn't have friends, because either I didn't fit in with them or they weren't on my level. It wasn't doing a lot of things that they were doing and that made me an outsider in their eyes. I was never the one that was trying to be popular, I was just one of those kids that just ended up being that way, not intentionally. I got more involved in high school and I guess it just happened. I was a model in junior high, I joined the choir, I signed up for ROTC and I did a lot of things, but still, I felt like I didn't belong. Still, I never had anyone I could talk to about what I was going through. Soon I started getting involved with stupid stuff, going through things I had no business going through at 15. I kind of lost focus at the time, these things happened before I decided to give my life to Christ at 15. I was going through all this extra stuff and ended up doing things I regret I ever done, being involved with guys doing things I shouldn't have did because I kept feeling like I was trying somewhere where I could fit in.

I couldn't talk to my mom about anything, I didn't have any friends really that I could talk to about anything and what I was going through. Being 15, I really didn't know myself what I was going through. I think I always been mature just in a younger body or something. I'll never forget that I got so depressed one day because I couldn't talk to anybody, and I never felt like what I was doing at that time, was helping, so I tried to commit suicide.

Heaven paused for a minute, so I asked if she needed any water or tea. She looked at me and said, "Yes, sweet tea would be great." I got up to go get her some iced tea and some Kleenex just in case she needed it and I got me a glass too. I sat back down in the recliner as she took a sip of her tea then she continued.

"I'm sorry Kris, were, was I? Oh yes, I tried to commit suicide."

With me being so crazy about the thought at the time with me not really knowing about what was going on with me and feeling so depressed, I went into my mother's bathroom and closed the door. I had found some pills that were in the medicine cabinet that belonged to my mom and I took them. The dumb part about it was I didn't pay attention to the pills I was taking before I took them. Evidently, it wasn't in God's plan for me to kill myself because when I realized I didn't die or get sick, I went back into my mother's medicine cabinet and notice that I took some vitamin pills! All I could do was look at myself in the mirror and laugh and just say, You're so Stupid! At the time it was just dealing with depression and not knowing how to handle it.

I leaned over and asked Heaven, "Did you know they were vitamins you were taking or was that the first thing you saw?" She laughed and said, "No! I didn't read what they were, I just opened the cabinet and grabbed the first bottle of pills I saw. I really thought I was doing something. I was young, I didn't sit and do research on the pills, I just took them. Young and dumb."

It was that Sunday, when God changed my life at the age of 15. That's when I felt like I belong to something bigger, something better, I felt like I could do more, I felt like He could use me more as a teenager to show people who He is because then, I wanted to learn.

God started to grow in me and grew up within me. My parents always made sure we went to church. It's not like it is now, when parents give their kids options if they want to go to church or not, no! you're going! My parents didn't play that mess. My mother Joann was a Sunday school teacher, so we had no choice but to go.

Heaven began to laugh while drinking her tea, so I asked a question.

"Heaven, was that rule for you or was it for everybody, your father as well?

Heaven stopped drinking and answered with the funniest laugh,

"Yes! All of us had to be there, it counted for everybody." As everyone started to get older, that's when we all started to fall off, leaving and going to other places, following their own path in life. For me, I stayed there the longest. As a teenager coming up, I remember I went out on my first date at the age of 16 and my mother was strict. After that first date, my mom didn't let me go out on another date until I was 17 years old and even then, my mother made me take one of my little sisters with me."

After hearing that, I had to stop the conversation an asked, "Why did she make you take your little sister? What happened on the first date for your mother to feel someone should go with you? Also, why take your little sister?"

She took another sip of tea, "Well me and one of my school friends went out and it really didn't even seem like a date because after I talked to him, I found out that the he was one of the those that wasn't what I thought he was. It was just me, I always felt that I was more mature then the other girls my age. I really wasn't felling him once I was out with him. It doesn't take me long to realize things about a person and how they act a certain way."

Can you elaborate on the reason why Joann let you go out on the first date alone, but not the second one and why you had to have someone with you?

Well the first one, we didn't go too far, we were close to the house and I guess mom felt safer. The second date was further away from the house, it was at a place they had for young people to hang out like a little club like scene. The guy that was taking me was a little bit older than me, so he got a friend that was around my sisters age to go. Hell, that date, I could have stayed at home too. It was terrible, I met him form a friend that stayed around the corner. We went to a place downtown and we talked and tried to get to know each other. The longer we talked, the more I realized this dude here was not for me. I found out he was an atheist. I was like HELL NO! I was ready to go home then, date over! Then I started to wake up even more, He didn't have his own ride to even take me out on a date then I find out he was an atheist. So, the conversation went from one thing to another.

I asked him, well who do you think woke you up this morning, who gave you the strength to get up in the morning? So, he said, "I got my own self up this morning, my alarm clock got me up!" So, I laughed and said, "Something wrong with you."

"That made me not date anymore guys my age, they were so stupid. Then it wasn't if my mom allowed it or not, I just chose not to. I really felt like they were not on my level anymore. It wasn't until I was 18 years old when I went out on my 3rd date, which turns out to be my last date. My last date I ever had, was with a guy that was four years older than me. I was 18 about to turn 19 soon and getting ready to graduate high school. I met him through a friend of mine from school. I was a senior and we cut class to go somewhere to eat and be back before anyone knew we were even gone. We would cut and I would go home and play sick when she asked me why I was home or tell her it was senior ditch day or something. I stopped after a while."

I stopped Heaven in her tracks and laughed, "You know this is going to get published, right? We both laughed and she continued.

Once I looked back at what I been through with the depression, attempted suicide, low self-esteem, and God, all lead up to where I was at that point in my life. I was 18 and I already felt that I went through hell and back. The things I went through at 15 years of age, had me fail the 9th grade, I was really depressed and alone. But I still felt a lot more mature at 18, things were so different now and I really don't know why I was so grown for my age. With every new experience, I learned something from all of it.

The last guy I dated, Garrison, everyone called him "OG" was a guy that my friend was supposed to hook him up with one of her other friends, but the other girl didn't show up. I really think my friend Tarra liked him and didn't want to admit it. Knowing her, she probably didn't even call the other girl to come hang with us."

Suddenly, I stopped the tape and I noticed Heaven started to look a bit flushed in the face. She had a look of sadness and hurt, she stopped talking and closed her eyes for a few seconds. I didn't say anything, I didn't do anything, so I just waited. I could tell something flashed across her mind that was about to be revealed but didn't know what.

When I met him, it was around Christmas time and he brought Tarra to my house to bring me a Christmas gift she had for me. They stayed right next door to each other, and she asked him could she bring her to my house to deliver my Christmas gift. He got out and he introduced himself to me and it was like love at first sight. We talked for a minute and we exchanged numbers. It just escalated from there. I was still trying to learn more about Christ and the best part about Garrison, he loved the Lord. I was still going through things and continuing my walk with Christ with no distractions and Garrison respected that. He ended up being my best friend I ever had. He was one of those men of God that had a gift of discernment, he told me I was going to be his wife before I knew he was going to be my husband. He took me to meet his mother, God rest her soul, I loved her to death.

How did he know you were going to be his wife? I asked.

Because he dated other women before, and he knew those women weren't for him. That moment when you feel that these other people just wasn't for you, like something in your gut tells you that something isn't right. Love is a feeling you get in your soul that runs through your veins with energy of hope and happiness. Sometimes you can be with a person and it just don't fit together, but we as women will try to make it work with a man who don't love us the same."

Once you get those feelings for a person, then you'll know if they are for you or not. Here is the tricky part about that, lust feels the same way. You can lust for a person and mistake it for love, many people don't know that. I truly believe a lot of relationships are built from lust. It kind of makes you want to analyze your relationships to see which one you're in.

"I'll never forget, his mother told me the he told her one time that the next woman he meets is going to be his wife and he was going to wait on God. Whenever I was with him, he never introduced me as his girlfriend, it was always as his wife. The stronger our relationship got, the more I knew he was my husband. The way our relationship started, it stared on Christ, it just the way it was put together. We prayed together, we went to church together, I would go to his church and he would come to mine. God was in this relationship all the way through and through. We were doing this, and we weren't even married! So, all I could do was wonder what our relationship would be like once we did get married. When I was going through things, he was the one that pulled me to the side and say let's pray, he was the one that said, God will get you through this. Garrison was a God send.

"We dated for about a year and three months and I was a virgin when I met him. He would come see me before he goes to work at 7am, before he went home from work and before he went to bed. People use to say, "why are you all so happy, we never hear or see you two argue and you two are always happy." I will admit, it was times where we did argue or have disagreements, but the secret was, we never put outside people in your business, we talked about it with each other and worked it all out with the help from God and that's all we needed.

A lot of relationships fail because we want to tell our family and friends what we are going through because we need someone to talk to sometimes. People hardly talk to God, the only One that will never tell you anything wrong or spread your personal issues all over the place. When you tell others everything you're going through, that's when you let the outside in. That's when you invite people who want to see you fail into your life, people who see how happy you are trying to come steal what you have and they become jealous and try to sabotage your relationship with lies, try to seduce your mate into being with them, and rumors begin to fly. Everyone can't be your friend and only a few can be your best friend. Women and men like that are unhappy and devilish, they can't stand to see others happy because they not happy and angry with themselves because of the decisions they made in life. Mad because they let that special someone go because they listened to other people and that is just petty."

When OG asked my dad to marry me, I was so blessed and excited that this man wanted to build a life with me. I loved him so much. OG was the type of man that admitted his faults, told me how he felt rather it be good or bad, and was always, always honest with me.

It was a time when we were engaged that he hit a rough patch and he felt like he wasn't going to be able to provide as a husband. He started to feel down on himself because the job where he was working at had close, so he went and found another job, that one closedown and went out of business. It was like every job he was working at either closedown or went out of business and he was started to feel that he couldn't provide for his wife and we weren't even married yet. I pulled him to the side one day and told him that God was still in the mist of this, but he felt that he didn't want to be a hindrance to my life, and he wanted to call off the engagement. He said, if he can't be an addition or a help meet to your life, then I refuse to be a subtraction or a hinderance to your life." That's when he felt like giving up. I keep telling him not to give up faith and keep trying and God will make a way out of no way. That's when I really didn't want to be a part of that if he didn't want to keep the faith and just felt like giving up this one time when the chips fail.

Heaven, have you ever thought about the fact that OG was feeling like that because he was about to be head of the household and he wasn't going to start a marriage off like that?

"Yes, I did think of that, could be, but we weren't married yet. This was about the time I was getting ready for PROM and I was about to take a trip to go see my Aunt in Wyoming for a little while. He had just bought my PROM dress and he took me to PROM when all this happened. His car had broken down and all this stuff was happening to OG and he was feeling really discouraged. I was getting ready to leave to go out of town and this man walked all the way to my house to see me off. My mom met him on the front porch and told him he better get it together before you lose this girl. It was so amazing because OG was standing on my porch crying and begging me not to break up with him. It was so loving to see that this man walked all the way to my house that I didn't even leave to go to my Aunts house, so I stayed. He was telling me not to give up on him and that we will get through this together. Things began to look up for us and we were getting things back on track. We told no one about our troubles, and God worked it out for our good.

Finally, we had gotten married later and end up having three kids out of all of this. We were more encouraging for each other than we thought. God puts people together because He knows they can help each other in trying times. The parts that you fall short of, He spiritually puts things back together.

Soon, he found another good job and I started working at the school system and started to attend college. As life went on, things began to be a bit overwhelming and I started to give up on faith and Garrison had to bring me back to reality with the word of God. That's what we called equally yoked.

We still hard trouble in our lives and in the mist of our troubles and how God blessed us with three wonderful children, it had gotten to the point where I couldn't do it anymore. I was working and going to school and raising three children and things started to take a toll on me. Despite of all of that, Garrison was there for those children. He made sure they went to school, ate, bathed, homework was done, and food was prepared when I got finally got home, then he went to work. He was such a good man and I adored him so very much.

He sat me down one day and said, "Lets pray, we are not going to let the devil win. Did you forget who God is? At, the time, I didn't want to take my own advice, but then I had to sit down and say, "Baby, you right, I forgot the same words I spoke over you, you just spoke over me." I started to get this renown strength over me and that's when I knew I could do this.

We made sure our kids didn't know all the financial things we went through, and we always tried to keep them happy. They never knew what we were going through, all they knew was mama and daddy was happy and we loved them. I realized how blessed I was because people can take things for granted sometimes and not focus on the things you are blessed with already. Despite of the things he was going through, OG always said we were blessed. Even the things he was going through with his side of the family. When thing started changing and began to get sick, he always kept God first in his life.

He started working for a construction company when I was pregnant with our second child the company he was working for, got bought out, he started to get frustrated. When he found out I was pregnant with our second child, he got very angry about it. Not that I was pregnant, but the changes he had to go through at this job, how is he going to take care of another child? At that time, our marriage was on the rocks, but still inside of all of that, I stayed encouraged because I was working and about to have our second child, he felt like I betrayed him. I know I can't get pregnant by myself, but he wasn't looking at all of that. How could we afford another child in the situation we were in? I was on birth control, but they were making me sick, so I stopped taking them. He was so angry with me, that he was trying to get a divorce because he just couldn't do it anymore.

Now, let me show you how God was still in control. I was about four months pregnant and he had an ex-girlfriend called me on my job to harass me, he had got just that angry. I was at work and it had got so nasty and evil, I had to step away and went and threw up at work. I couldn't believe he would do that. I was so upset to the point I called his mom and when she found out, she let him have it and then on top of that, it was time for our anniversary and his birthday coming up. When I got home, I started praying, he asked me for a divorce, and I wasn't going to give him one. So, I went and got him something for his birthday because I was not going to let the devil win over my family.

I got him something nice for his birthday, had dinner ready when he got home and ran him a nice hot bath for when he got there, and a gift for him.

"Heaven? Wait a minute." I paused to clear my head for a minute because all I could do was imagine the perfect murder scene. "You know this book is getting published, do I need to stop recording before we go any further?"

We both laughed, "I think I seen this episode in a movie before, it didn't end well for the man."

She looked at me and started laughing and said, "No Kris! It's not that type of story!"

I looked at her and said, "OK, just checking."

Garrison couldn't look me in my eyes the whole time. Once he was done, he got up and went into the living room and asked me, "Why did I do that? So, I turned to him and said first and for most, you are my husband, when I married you, it was for sickness and in health, for better or for worst, till death do us part. You are my husband and I am sticking to my vows."

Did he check his food?

"No, I wasn't that crazy, I could have been, but I wasn't. I fear God over man. I bought him an outfit and some shoes for his birthday and that's when he fell to the floor to ask for forgiveness." While he was crying, I asked him did him and this young lady happen to have an affair? She was that type of woman who was after men with money, she'll go after any man that will benefit her and don't care if they are married or not. If she felt like it would benefit her, then she would do whatever it takes to get that man. And she wonders why her life is like it is. She raised her three daughters the same way, it's a shame. The funny part about it is she older than me.

Anyway, he said, "I did it because I was hurt. I wanted you to want the divorce and she was the only person I could think of that would do it. I never touched her, I just felt betrayed and I thought I was getting the upper hand."

I leaned down next to him and said, "Don't you know God doesn't put no more on you that you can bare? No burden is to hard or too impossible for God! Did you forget that?" He looked up at me and said, "Obviously I forgot, I was so blind with anger, I couldn't see it. Please forgive me!"

I looked at him and said, "You know what, since you want this divorce, I'll give it to you."

"Heaven, are you sure he was saying that because he felt you might hurt him while he slept? I mean, it's sound just like a Lifetime movie or something, I'm just saying. I bet you was talking to him with a smile on your face, wasn't you? Come on now, food, bath water, new outfit and shoes, then you told him you were going to give him the divorce. Really? That's a whole other book right there! Well that's what I got out of it."

"Well Kris, no, I love my husband and we were going to pull through this with my faith and strength in God. He told me that he didn't deserve me. He kept saying please forgive me. I assured him that I will raise those kids with or without him, but he got to remember God is in control."

When Cherish was born, she was a big peachy fat baby, we were staying in a duplex off Baldwin street and we were blessed to move to a house that had three bedrooms. Once again, God has blessed us so we could move into a bigger home with more space. After we moved in, I anointed everything of his all the way down to his shoes and I told God that I was giving my husband back to His hands, and He did. I started to see a huge change in Garrison, he had become the man I fell in love with at the age of 18 all over again.

The same baby he thought he didn't want; was the same baby he couldn't live without. He loved all his kids equally but the bond between him and Cherish was different. Maybe because of what we went through when I was pregnant with her brought him closer to her and her to him in the womb.

OG had just gotten a new job and I finally went into labor with Cherish. My husband had already started working and he wanted to come to the hospital, but I told him not to because he had just started working there. Luckily, the company was understanding, and they allowed him to come. My husband has always loved kids, he wanted kids before he even thought about getting a wife. OG was always the type of person that would give his shirt off his back just to help those in need.

After having Cherish, we were still in the three-bedroom home in pretty good neighborhood and life was well, until a lady with six kids moved in and stared causing issues on the street we were on. We lived in a cove and at the time, this woman was friendly but apparently had a bad reputation with the fellas and her kids caused so much trouble. So, one day, our house got broken into and the lady had a daughter that always spoke to me, she said that her mama's friends went into your house and got some of your stuff. I looked in disbelief and I called my husband and work, when he came home, he said he saw a man selling things that looked like ours on the corner at the gas station one blocks away. We asked God for the strength to confront these people but for some reason, they just upped and moved away. God still replaced everything that was stolen from us, I don't know how God did it, but He did.

So, a few weeks had passed by and another woman named Amber moved in the same house (maybe it's a bad spirit in that house or something) and drama came with that lady as well. See, she was the type of woman that ask men to do things for her in return for a sexual favor. You'll see different guys at her house most of the time especially at night. Well, this day, she was outside, and my husband was doing yard work with our kids, so she walked over and asked him could he give her a ride to the grocery store so her kids can have something to eat. He told her he would just as soon as he puts up his tools and he will get his kids so they could ride with them.

(Mind you, I knew nothing about this until I got home from visiting my mother's house since she was ill.)

He ended up taking to the store and he sat in the car with our kids and waited for her to come out. In about 45 minutes she returned to the car with no grocery bags, so he asked her, "I thought you was going grocery shopping? We been out here waiting for you for almost 45 minutes." She smiled and him and said, "I did go shopping but I saw another friend of mines in the store and I put the groceries in his car because he was going to take me back home, but we need to make another stop and I didn't want you to wait."

Garrison looked at the lady and said ok, "God bless you." Right when he got ready to pull off, Amber said, "Is your wife home OG?" he said, "No, but she is on her way home now. Why?" Amber turned and looked at OG and said, "Aw, ok, I was going to get you to come to my house so you can get payment for taking me to the grocery store." Then she licked her lips. My husband told her "Just count it as a blessing and no payment is needed" and he pulled off.

"When I got home, he told me everything, all the way down to that woman licking her lips at him. I laughed for a minute and then my anger tried to kick in. We prayed for her and her family and left it up to the Lord to handle her. One day, my husband had to take his mom to the doctor, and he was gone for a while. Amber's kids came down to my house trying to start stuff with my daughters and they came all up on my porch yelling and cursing. That's when I went outside, and I confronted the children and told them to go back home and don't come on my porch anymore with that mess. One of the kids turned and yelled out F you Lady! and they all laughed, so, I put God on hold for about 5 minutes and I went into my bedroom and grabbed my husband's walking cane and I came back to the porch and said, "You have 1.2 seconds to get off my porch and never come back here or bother my kids again!" All the kids ran off the porch screaming and yelling "MAMA!"

"At that time Kris, I didn't think about nothing spiritual related because they had crossed the line with me. They threated my children, they were on my property and I felt violated by their presents, enough side. Everyone has that moment in life were God is the last thing on your mind right now, depending on how bad the issues are. God can be the last person on your list when things going down and that was one of them for me. You just have to ask for forgiveness later. Hell, I was pisst!"

I'm human and sometimes we step out of Godly ways and react to our emotions. I would never do anything to harm anyone's child but at that moment those little creatures were pushing it. I had to do something to get them off my porch. Of course, the mother did not come down the street or say anything about what happened, I guess because she had stuff going on at her house that she didn't want the police involved anyway. Amber did try to get back at us for it though.

She had two of her sons take their lawn mower and put it in our yard somewhere where we couldn't see it and called the police and told them that my husband stole they lawnmower, my husband wasn't even home when that happened, he was at work. When the police came to my door and asked about the lawnmower being in our yard, I told them we had our own lawnmower and I took them to the back for them to see it and that's when I saw another mower sitting off to the side of the shed. I told the officers that that was not our mower but the one in the shed was. Right then, my husband came home and saw the cops there and they questioned him and got ready to take him to jail. The whole time, Amber was standing on the sidewalk with this devilish look on her face while her kids grabbed the mower and pushed it back down to her house. My husband was so confused about everything he didn't know what to do. Then Amber yelled out, "He wanted me to sleep with him for taking me to the grocery store two weeks ago and I felt uncomfortable, so I got another friend to take me home and he got mad. That's probably why he stole my mower!"

"Kris, do you know the whole time, this female had a smile on her face, and she was holding a little girl that had flies flying around her diaper while she was running her mouth? How do you stay in a holy spiritual mindset when you looking the devil in his face? I closed my eyes and prayed on the spot that God hold me down because this female was about to meet Jesus personally. I mean, the rage that was growing in me was so powerful to the point it scared me. Then I heard God say, "Peace" and I knew then that He had this taken care of, but I still wanted to give the Lord a little push, you know, like a running start.

Once it was all over, Garrison had to go to court to try and clear his name. It went on for months, by the time all this was coming to an end, I was pregnant with my third child Grant. I assume with all that's going on and him trying to fight it and seeing how long all this was taking, GG had missed a court date and they issued a bench warrant for him. I believe he stayed down there for three days, but we got him out with help with family members. By the time he got out, Amber and her tribe had moved away. I don't know what it was about that street or that house she was in, but every time someone moved in it, it was always something going on with that family.

As time went on, we moved out of the house and had to move in with his mom. We bought that house as is and it had become too much to bare after a while. It was a good thing because his mom had had a hard life and time was creeping up on her. His mom, Gloria Gates, had a hard life, her mom put her out at 18, she was raped and abused and by the time she married Garrison's dad, it got even worst. Garrison Gates Sr., everyone called him Garry because he didn't like his own name. Garry abused his wife by beating her and making her sale herself on the streets to make money. He began to help his mom take care of herself plus working and taking care of his own family, started to take a toll on him. His brothers and sisters didn't help because of other health and personal reasons, and when he needed them the most, they were nowhere to be found. Isn't it amazing how people can bend over backwards for you and when it's time for help for yourself, all you hear is silence.

As time went on, we got a new place to live and everything was going well. The kids were getting bigger and some of the stresses in life was getting to be under control. But now we had a new hurdle to jump, my husband health problems started to increase. He had an enlarged heart, migraine headaches that would bring him to his knees, and high blood pressure. With him being a man, he would have to be reminded to take his medicine, eat right, and keep his stress level to a minimum. He was being stubborn most times thinking that he didn't need all those medicines saying, "I feel just fine all day until I start taking that medicine, that's when I start feeling bad after it kicks in!"

Arguing with him about taking that medicine was like trying to convert a Cowboys fan into a Steelers fan, it just ain't going to work. It was times were he really needed it and he finally gave in and took it. At this point, he had stopped working and applied for disability because his health issues had gotten to be frequent, at first it would hit him every so often and by then, it was almost every day.

Our oldest daughter Destiny was twelve now, Cherish was eleven and Grant was six when things started to get overwhelming with his health. When his health changed for the worst, we were getting up to take the kids to school and Cherish walked in the room to wake him up just like she did every morning and she said, "Momma, wake up, something wrong with Daddy!"

Heaven paused and didn't say anything for about 5 minutes. "Heaven, do you want to stop? We don't have to put this part in the book if you don't want too." I walked over to her and laid my head on her shoulder and she whispered a little prayer to herself. I heard her say, "Heavenly farther, give me strength to continue on, let my story help someone in the world, if just one person can learn from this, then I would have done my part."

Once she said that, she looked at me and said, "Your book is going to help so many women and I am proud to be a part of it."

With my heart melting on the inside, I went a grabbed her some Kleenex, gave her the biggest huge a best friend could give another friend and said, "Let Him use you Heaven Gates. We can stop at any time if you feel you can't go on with this."

I really didn't know what was about to happen next and I didn't know if I was prepared for it, but God be the Glory. She sat up and collected herself and she began to speak. Her voice was saddened, her spirit had fallen but her strength as a strong woman kicked in. It was priceless and I was very grateful to have seen this in person, the power of God working through her right before my eyes. She was my friend and I am proud to call her my best friend in the world.

Where was I, oh, yes, Cherish had come into the room and said that something was wrong with her daddy. When I woke up, I turned over and looked at him, his eyes had rolled to the back of his head and he was unresponsive, so I jumped up and said, "Oh My God!! He's having a stroke!!" I got up and called 911 and then called his brother Gerry to rush him to the hospital. I remember a long time ago, he told me that he wasn't going to live to see 40 years old and that he had already seen my death. I asked him how did he know that and why would he say that? Evidently, the Lord must have showed it to him. Now I see why he kept trying to prepare us for that moment, but I thought it was just him being cautious. I always told him to quit talking like that, we are going to be ok and we will be sitting on the porch watching our grandkids play one day. Sadly, that day never came for him. He was 35 years old when he had the stroke. I had to help him do everything all over again, the stroke messed up a part of his brain that dealt with the memory. Once again, we had to move out the house we were in and move back in with his mom because I didn't know how to drive so his siblings help me take him back and forth to the doctors' offices and so forth.

After a while, he started going downhill from there, we were still trying to apply for Social Security Disability and I really don't know why in the bloody hell that stuff takes so long? While we were trying to make ends meet, they still wanted more proof of his disability and I think that is a damn shame! What does a person have to do? Die! before they declare someone disable?! Sorry.

OG had begun to lose so much weight and he would always say how tired he was, by this time, he was 36 years old. We had to sleep in separate beds, we were in the same room but separate beds because he needed so much help to get out of the bed and to the rest room. Sometimes he didn't want to bother me trying to get up, so he slept in another bed. Even while he was sick, he still thought about others. How many men are like that now? I know it's some out there, but it can be more. So many people take life for granted.

That morning, he woke up and said, "Baby, something doesn't feel right." I turned to him and asked what was wrong. "My left arm, it feels funny." I jumped up and said, "G! I think you're having a heart attack!"

I got up and got someone to take us to the ER, I could have called the ambulance, but we couldn't afford to wait for one and we had a car outside. By this time, it was 2001, the year that changed my life, by this time, Destiny was 13, Cherish was 11, and Grant was 6 and we all rushed to the hospital with him. After they put him in a room, he told me to go check on his mother, brother and the kids. I felt so bad for leaving him in the room, but he insisted that I go check on the rest of the family to make sure they were holding it together. Sadden, I didn't want to step out because I knew they were about to come get him to run more tests on him and I didn't want to miss a thing. But, to make him happy, I said ok, if that would keep his stress level down knowing that his kids and his mom knew he was ok. Before I left the room, Garrison looked at me and grabbed my hand and said, "Baby, I love you." I looked at him and said, "I love you too Garrison Gates." And I walked out.

Meanwhile, we were all waiting in the waiting room while they had him upstairs for tests and this nurse came out and escorted us all to the Chapel. Me being me, I looked at her and said, "Umm... why are we here. What happened?! The nurse politely said, Mrs. Gates, he didn't make it. I'm so sorry. I'm going to go get the doctor to explain what going on."

The doctor came in the room and told us when they took him upstairs to run test on him to see what was going on with him and was that a heart attack he just had earlier, that's when he died. The heart attack gave him a blood clot, with all the other issues going on in his body with the enlarged heart, or Congestive Heart Failure, I don't know because we haven't heard of any of those conditions before, it all just took him out of here, he died.

When they told me, all I remember was hitting the floor, I fell to my knees and started crying. I just lost my best friend, how was I going to tell his children that daddy wasn't coming home with me? They had gone back to his mother's house earlier while we waited for results from the tests and now I had to call them and tell them that their farther had died, how do you make a call like that and you're not there to comfort your babies?

Heaven stopped talking and started crying even harder, the love and hurt she had on her face made me cry with her because she never told me in detail what happened with her husband. As long as we've been friends, I never brought the subject up because I didn't want her to relive that moment. As I held her, her tears were flowing down her face and I felt her getting weak. I never seen this strong black woman break down like she did. I looked up to her, she was my strength when I was weak, my prayer warrior when I fell and needed to be lifted with God's word, my thug when I was ready to clap back at someone, and my sister in Christ. I loved here.

I got up and ran to get her a cup of water, but that didn't quench her thirst, I went into the bathroom and got her more tissue, but that didn't dry her tears, I ran to the cabinet to get her some popcorn or crackers, but that didn't feed her hunger. So, I ran to my husband and he gave me a scripture to read to her to quench her thirst, to dry her tears, to feed her hunger and to heal her heart.

"Peace I leave with you; My peace I give to you.

I do not give you as the world gives.

Do not let your hearts Be Troubled

And do not be afraid."

John 14:27

Heaven took a few moments to herself while we tried to sip on some soda and I noticed after I read the scripture, she looked up at me and said, "Garrison died on his mother's birthday and we buried him on our son birthday, Grant was turning seven. It was September 26, 2001 when he died, and we buried him on the 29th of that month. I couldn't do it anymore, I have lost all since of reality, I wanted to get it over with. My heart has been torn out of my body, my soul has separated from me and my lifeline has expired, he was my air and he left me."

"I WANTED TO DIE, I FORGOT THAT I HAD KIDS, I FELT LIKE I WAS dreaming, and I had lost all the feeling in my body. But that wasn't anything compared to the anger and rage I had towards God. I wanted to know what was His purpose for taking my husband away from me, away from his kids, and away from his family? On his mother's birthday for Christ sake! Really!? I wanted to know why! Why did He do this to me?! Why did He take him from us?! What kind of God is this?! A God who tells you to be a family, but He takes the family away from you! I was furious!"

Somebody told me one day that God won't put no more on you that you can bare, or something like that. The person who said it has a nice life with all her family still together. Don't you hate getting encouraging words from people who seems to have everything going well in their life but have the nerve to tell you what you feeling is ok? The thing I hate the most is when someone tells you, "Everything is going to be ok." I hate that, like, I just lost my husband and you out on a date with your husband and you got the nerve to tell me it's going to be ok? Girl!! Get off my phone! That's what you want to say sometimes. But, you can't because all you can say is thank you. Then here is on that gets on my everlasting nerve, "I'll pray for you." "Really?" I don't like that, if you going to pray for me then do it right then, and you know darn well you haven't spoken to God about anything you going through so what makes me believe that person is really praying for me? If you tell me you're going to pray for me, then let's do it right then and there. That was my mindset for a while, what can I say, I'm human.

I was so angry, and my mom talked to me through scripture. She said "you must go on and you have to live for these kids. I know your angry right now, but you have to remember Heaven, God don't make no mistakes." Then I said, "Well mama I know, but He did this time."

As I glanced over at Heaven, the hurt on her face came back all over again. I jumped up and sat next to her and she began to cry even harder. After what she said about people comforting her, I didn't know what to do but hold her and cry with her. I started to realize that no matter what we all go through in life, nothing can comfort you better than comforting yourself. I gave her a scripture, I gave her love, I offered her peace to stop the pain by ending this part of her story. What else can I do? I remembered one time, I had a loving friend that just lost is sister and my way of comforting him was just to be quite and listen. No one knew how to comfort him, but for some reason, I did. As his anger towards God got bigger and bigger, his cousin walked up to me and asked to calm him down. How could

I calm him down? Him and his brother just lost their only sister. Well, the same thing I did with him, I did for my friend Heaven. I held her and didn't say a word, I let her vent just like I let him vent. After an hour or so, we sat there and didn't say anything for about 20 minutes. He lit a cigarette and said thank you while wiping the tears from his eyes. That's when I realized that being quiet and letting them vent is the best medicine for those in a traumatic life changing moment. I held Heaven and I didn't say a word, I waited until she was ready to talk again.

"For a while I always held on to the little hope in my life. When he died, my life went out of control. I wasn't living like I was supposed to, and I knew it, I was trying to fill that void in my life that was once filled with a man that I truly loved, and I couldn't find it anymore. I was trying to replace what I had lost. In the middle of me doing that, I made some dumb choices and mistakes that I asked God to forgive me for, the mean things I said towards the Lord, for yelling at God, and for saying He made a mistake. I realize I couldn't do it by myself. Years after my husband passed away, I started living in the world. I was dating guys, being intimate with them and I was just spiraling out of control. I had lost all faith."

As she held her head down, I decided to ask her a question. "How did you finally make peace with God? I know how you feel to a certain extent because I have been mad with God a few times in my life, especially when every time I tried to do right and live right, things got worst. No matter what I did, nothing got better and praying felt like it wasn't working. My question to you is, what happened for you to finally make peace with everything and how your anger felt towards God?

Well, my anger towards him was so strong, because my son needed his father and with Grant being just six years old at the time, I felt that he wasn't going to have that Godly man in his life that he would need growing up. I was angry because God was wrong for that. How could He do that to my son? Yes, I had five brothers and a father, and he had two uncles on his daddy side, who is going to help him stay on the right path to guide him into manhood? God took the only hope my son had in his life, I could only teach him so much. I can't teach him how to be the man he needs to be. At that point in my life, I couldn't hear God anymore, I didn't have the ear to hear Him like I use to. He didn't answer my prayers, He didn't hear me when I called out to Him, so I said forget it all together, let the chips fall where they lay.

The pastor of the Church I was attending at that time said that I had to find peace, God don't make mistakes. I looked at him and said, "How can I find peace in this?" then he said, "Garrison's mission was completed, and the Lord called him home. Yes, you needed him here, but God needed him more. We do not have a choice when it is our time to go. When the Father calls His angles home, do you think we can argue with God? No."

I CAME TO THE CONCLUSION, AND HOW I FOUND PEACE, WAS when I realizes that God will take away things from you when we lose sight of Him. We as people can be so caught up in the material things we have, the things we work hard to get, the love of our life we try so hard to keep, that car, that house, that success etc. we lose site of the big picture. His death brought the entire family closer together because God knows our story and if we don't embrace life with God in it, then humanity is lost. Also, God is the one who blessed you with what you have. God had to take him away. OG was sick and once I got out of my feelings for years, I realized that I would rather for God to take him then to see him suffer like he was. I was being selfish and tried to keep him here with me. How I know if Garrison told God he was ready to go once I left out the room that day he died. Maybe my husband prayed and asked God to take him away, so he won't be a burden on us while we tried to take care of him. No one knows that but OG and God. We don't know what other people pray for in secret. Garrison made a difference in other people's lives and I truly believe once we pass our tests with God, then He'll call us home. Everyone must go one day, rather you believe in God or not, we all must face Him and give account for the way we lived. Your friends won't be there with you on judgement day, your spouse won't be there, your job won't be there, that crew you ran the streets with won't be there to get you out of the face of God. We can't blame anything on anyone else because it's our responsibility to stand before Him alone and answer the questions the Lord will ask us, and He will be the final judge to see if we are going to live in paradise with Him or live in Hell. God gives us choices and the mercy of forgiveness.

SEPTEMBER IS A VERY HARD MOTH FOR US. MY HUSBAND PAST IN September, his baby brother died in September and his birthday is the 27th of September and he died from a triple aneurism. My son birthday is in September which is the anniversary of the day we buried my husband. His mother's birthday is on the 26th and she passed in December and she was in her 70's. It was so much to handle, but life went on and my children and I are closer than ever and my faith in God has been restored. I gave up on God, but He never gave up on me.

My advice to other women is never lose faith, despite of the storm, no matter how it looks, it will always get better. Rather you are just entering the storm or coming out of the storm, God will always be there with you. Keep your eyes on Him and pray your way out of it. The bible says, "If you ask for anything in My name, it will be yours." John 14

To those who don't believe in God and to the ones who won't take the time to pray like they supposed to because you're comfortable with the way your living, I really hope that all the women in this book that told their story, one of them had to speak to you. God is Love and He will never turn His back to you. Even though you might feel that God doesn't hear you or He is allowing bad things to happen to you, you must know that it's not how the story can end in your life. God listens to everything you say, He just wants to see how long it's going to take for you to give in. He will never force us to believe in Him or His Son Jesus Christ, free will remember? Try saying thank you every day and see how things can change. Don't only call on Him when somebody in your life has been taken away, don't just call on Him when you need a bill paid or a house or car you want. Call on Him all the time and give him thanks all the time, even for the little things and see how things will change. Let go of those people in your life that are causing harm to you mentally and physically. If you ever notice how things happen when you hang around certain people, or that feeling you get right before you about to do something and you know it's not right? That's Him. That little voice in your head or what some people say, "I should have followed my first mind." That's the Holy Ghost, that little voice that sounds like you in your head is Him. We can tell people tell people to give God a chance until we are blue in the face, they will have to get to Him on they own and not when things have totally gotten out of control. We all want to call on God at the last minute, He is not a last-minute God or a genie in a lamp that you can rub every time you need saving. That must come from within and if you not praying at all, you better find something to pray too. When your life is at the end of its rope, you need to give God a try. Don't wait until you take care of it yourself, yes, it might go well but everything has its consequences. God said in Matthew 6; 26 -32

Look at the birds of the air; they do not sow or reap or store away in barns, and yet your heavenly Father feeds them. Are you not much more valuable than they? Can any one of you by worrying add a single hour to your life? "And why do you worry about clothes? See how the flowers of the field grow. They do not labor or spin.

Yet I tell you that not even Solomon in all his splendor was dressed like one of these. If that is how God clothes the grass of the field, which is here today and tomorrow is thrown into the fire, will he not much more clothe you-you of little faith? So do not worry, saying, 'What shall we eat?' or 'What shall we drink?' or 'What shall we wear?'

"IF WE CAN LIVE BY THIS SCRIPTURE ALONE, I GUARANTEE YOU that things will work out for you, but you have to give Him a chance. People need to give God at 30 days. Everyone wants to do all these weird challenges on YouTube and Facebook, do a 30 of God only challenge and see what happens, I promise you, you will see a difference in your life. So, to all the women out there, I leave you with the last part of Matthew 6: 32-34 and I bet you, it will change your life. My name is Heaven Gates, and this is my story. God be with you all, stay blessed.

MATTHEW 6; 32 -34

For the pagans run after all these things, and your heavenly Father knows that you need them. But seek first his kingdom and his righteousness, and all these things will be given to you as well. Therefore do not worry about tomorrow, for tomorrow will worry about itself. Each day has enough trouble of its own.

CHAPTER 7
GRACE AND MERCY
THE TWINS

"All our lives we believed God had a hilarious since of humor. One minute our lives are in total turmoil, and the next, God is pouring down blessings where you don't have enough room to receive it. Back and forth and back and forth people lives are spinning out of control. But, when it's all said and done, we still give God all the praise. Through the good times and the bad, we are supposed to thank Him through it all, well, some of us do. Me, I praise God every chance I get, from the living room to the garage to get in my car to go to work. I thank Him not only for the big things, but for the very small things too. For example, I say thank you for letting me safely pass from one lane to the other on the express way and not getting mowed over by a speeder who is late for work. I thank Him for letting me have ramen noodles for dinner instead of being hungry at night. I thank Him for letting me brush my teeth every day and not having to have someone do it for me because I'm incapable to do it due to failing health or a physical disability. I thank Him for letting me drive to the closet Walgreens to get dish soap and make it back home the same way I left, in one piece. If we thank Him for the little things as much as we thank Him for the bigger things, then He will know that we greatly and humbly appreciate Him for everything, good or bad but, not all of us are that grateful.

Our names are Grace and Mercy and we are identical twins, this is our story.

My name is Grace Givens, everyone calls me GG, all my life everyone called me Good Girl because of my nickname GG. My father came up with our names Grace and Mercy when we were born, we came out too early and my mother Gabby M. Givens, was experiencing severe complications during childbirth and they had to do an emergency C-section. Unfortunately, our mother died as soon as we were delivered, July 7th, 1977. My mom started running a high fever which set up infection and soon after, she passed away. The doctors told my father if they didn't get us out soon, we were going to die as well. After many tests and medications, gratefully we pulled through. My father told me that he asked God to show him grace and mercy because he can't handle the fact of all three of his loves dying on the same day, and that's when he decided to name us Grace and Mercy Givens.

My dad, Josh Givens, was a wonderful man and father. He raised us alone here in Indianapolis with a little help from his sister, Angel Givens. He made sure we knew all about our mother our entire lives and on July 7th of every year, he told us the story about how we got our names and how God showed him grace and mercy because He didn't take us from him. July 7th is the day we were born and the day my mother died so we always celebrated with a fancy dinner and photos of her and us growing up. It was always a bittersweet occasion, dad would laugh all night then cry himself to sleep, I wondered how he did it all those years, especially when we look just like our mother.

My dad had us in all the church events and programs, in school, he made sure we stayed busy with soccer, tennis, and the drama club. He always said I had a wild and unusual imagination. As for Mercy, she loved the drama club, but the sports, not so much. Since we were identical twins, we would switch out sometimes during the activities and no one ever caught on, not even our dad. So, we weren't always good girls, especially Mercy, that girl did everything in secret, she was very clever in her schemes to get over on people, sometimes she'll even fool me. She could do something and convince me that I was there with her the whole time, how good is that? And I believed it!"

"Mrs. Kris, I am sorry Mercy isn't here to tell any parts of our story, we both agreed to do it in honor of our father and our mother. For some reason, she decided not to show her face today because she didn't want to go back down memory lane with me. She said that our dad did enough storytelling to write his own Netflix series."

As I wrote down Grace's words, I noticed she stopped talking. When I looked up, Grace was staring off into space like she remembered something dreadful. Her eyes were glazed over, and her hands started shaking. I looked up at her and said, "Well, you'll be a star if this did go to Netflix." Then I laughed. When I said that, she snapped out of whatever trance she was in and started laughing and said, "No ma'am, cast me as Angela Bassett or Queen Latifah, I'm not putting my face on nobodies screen." We both laughed for a minute and then she offered me some lemonade.

Grace got up from her couch and walked towards the kitchen, as she walked away, I looked around her room and couldn't help but notice pictures of her and her dad. Not one picture of her twin sister Mercy. Maybe they had a fallen out and that's why she is telling her story, maybe her father loved her more than Mercy, or, Mercy was in some of those pictures and I just didn't notice it because they are identical twins. Only Grace can tell me, so I better not ask.

Grace came out of the kitchen with a pitcher of pink lemonade and two glasses on a silver platter and placed them in front of me. As she sat down, I reached down into my brief case to get out more paper so we can begin. Grace stood up and got ready to pour me some lemonade and in the process of her pouring, she looked up at me with a smile and said, "See, we all have a story to tell, it's up to the reader who's story they want to believe." I smiled at her and said, "Your right GG, people will believe what they want to believe. The truth can be staring them right in the face and they wouldn't even know it. They choose to see what they want to see."

She looked at me and said, "Your right Kris" she said with a grin, "People don't realize that everything isn't what it seems. Now, let's begin shall we."

For some reason, I felt a creepy feeling going through my veins. Like something off a horror film right before someone gets murdered. I put my glass down and picked up my pen and began to write. I prayed to God for GG to get her thoughts together so we can have a good meeting, whatever she is about to say, I pray that it would help someone who is struggling with something like what she is about to tell me. I took another sip of lemonade and said, "Ready?". She looked at me and said, "Ready?" then she began.

"From the time I was little, I always knew I was different from other kids. My friends use to call me Godly, holier than thou, and daddy's girl. It was ok with me because their fathers were friends with my dad, so we all had the same upbringing. But it was times where they would back off from me and play with Mercy instead of me. Maybe they didn't know that they were hanging with her and not me, Mercy and I played little games like that sometimes. Especially when I didn't feel like being bothered that day.

As Mercy and I grew up, she became closer to our friends and farther away from me and dad. The only person who could keep up with her was my Auntie Angel. Seems like she always knew how to tell us apart and who broke something in the house. You will meet her later; she will be over this evening to bring me some paperwork that we have to look over. Anyway, we had a great childhood, my dad did the best he could raising us with the help of my Auntie. Angel taught us all the women stuff like menstrual cycles and how to be a smart independent woman. My dad taught us the difference between a boy and a man, how to fix on our own cars, yard work, house maintenance and all the things an independent woman should know. He told us to get as much education we could get if we are on this earth. He said people should never stop learning new things because we will never know what life will throw at us. He even taught us how to speak Spanish because he said if we can speak Spanish, we can land more jobs. My sister and I are lawyers for a major law firm, and we make pretty good money for ourselves.

Now that you have a brief history about us, now I can tell you how God helped us in our lives. Mercy agreed to tell her side through me because she always was the type of person that kept to herself even though she had more friends than me. We might be identical twins but when it comes to God, we are two totally different people. I never asked her why she was the way she was, maybe because a part of me was like her too. My father accepted it and my aunt wanted to change it for the better. I always wondered was God a myth, a fairy tale to keep people in order, or a real God. My sister on the other hand, didn't care one way or another. She used to always say that our minds are our pathway to life's greatest adventure, if we think it hard enough, it will come to past. But I always told her if we pray for it hard enough, it will come to past in God's timing. Then she will argue that if the world can grow a human in a pastry dish, then we can change our own life's path in the blink of an eye. I guess that's why she is a successful lawyer because she can argue with the devil and convince him into putting the fire out. She always said that if you get on the devils nerve long enough, he will leave you alone, but we must worry God day and night just to get one prayer answered. I don't know if that girl is an atheist or a saint. It's funny because she can turn an atheist into a Christian and a Christian into an atheist. I had to ask that girl whose team was she playing on because she confuses the hell out of me at times. Damn girl is bat crazy, but she's my sister and I love her. I don't know if you should put that part in your book or not. The name of your book is "The Daughters of God" but I don't know if your readers would even like that part."

As I looked at Grace, I smiled at her and said, "I can take that part out if you want me too, it's your story and I will write whatever you want me too. All you have to say to me is you want this off the record and I won't put it in the there. I will not document anything you don't want to say, I promise." She giggled and said, "Well it's the truth so you can leave it in there. It is what it is."

"Now, where was I? oh... yes, back to my story." Mercy and I did everything together from picking our clothes to wear, all the way down to our monthly duties. In school, it was times where I had to go urinate and before I could ask the teacher could I be excused, I'll see Mercy already walking down the hall to go to the restroom too. It's like, I could feel her and know if she was hurt or sick and we wouldn't have to be in the same room or in the same house. One day Mercy and I was bored so we went to the computer and started googling identical twins and everything they said twins do, we did. It was amazing that we weren't the only ones feeling like this. Mercy and I thought we had superpowers when we were little because I could think of something and she would do it, same goes for me. I can think about going to get me a soda while I was doing homework and within minutes, she would have brought us both a soda. Once we read about the twins and how alike some of us are, we were happy that we weren't the only ones with magical powers, as we called it. Until......"

GG stopped talking and began to shift in her seat. Whatever she was about to say apparently made her uncomfortable.

"Let me tell you why I agreed to be in your book. It might sound unbelievable to some and breath taking to others. I am going to tell you the day my sister and I saw the face of God."

As Grace prepared herself, she received a phone call. She asked could we pause for a minute and I said sure. While she took her phone call, I got up and excused myself to go to the restroom before we got started again. As I walked through her home, pictures of herself with family members were all in the hallway along the walls towards her bathroom. I thought to myself if she really had a close relationship with her sister like she says she does. I'm just going to ask her when I get back, I thought to myself.

After using the restroom, I walked back to her living room and I heard Grace say, "Come by if you want, it would be great for you to meet Mrs. Kris. I have already told her about you. Maybe you could give a little input on this story." Then I heard her say, "Yes, I am going to tell what happened, I think it would be good for her readers. It would be nice to let other women know that they aren't alone."

As she got ready to end her called, I sat back in the chair and grabbed my paper and pen. Scratching my head at the same time wondering what this story is going to be about.

"Ok" she said, "See you shortly, love you, bye-bye."

She looked over at me with a huge smile and said, "Sorry about that, but we will have a visitor come join us later, I hope that's ok?" I smile and said, "Sure, the more the merrier! But will we have to stop? I know this is supposed to be a book with everyone's identity covered, will that interfere with what we are doing? If so, I can hide all of my things and make it look like I'm just visiting." GG waved her hands and said, "No, that will be unnecessary, she knows what I am doing, and she won't say a word, I trust her."

I looked at her and smiled and said, "Ok, great." I grabbed my pen and waited until she spoke again.

"I truly believe women are the strongest creatures on the face of the earth. Don't get me wrong, men are strong and powerful beings too, but their strength is a little different than ours. All through history, men were looked at as the bread winners, the providers, the security, the head of the house, the comforters, the lovers, and the decision makers. I respect all of that about a man because my father was every-thing and more. But a woman, a woman can be all those things as well and more. It's just a different kind of power, a power that only a woman can feel, and I truly believe that's how God made us to be. We can literally feel the love of a tiny little

human growing in us. Babies are attached to us physically and emotionally, just like how twins are. Think about it, being pregnant is just like having a twin, they do everything together. They eat, sleep, laugh, cry, and praise God together because that's how God bounds you together with your baby. Falling in love at first sight with someone you never met before, you never seen that child before and you instantly fall in love when you see them. Isn't that like Jesus? We never met Him, we never seen Him, never spoke to Him face to face, but we love Him with all the breath in our bodies. He comforts us when we feel down, we see His glory and love through different life experiences, we feel Him through praise and worship, and He is always showing up in His timing, just like babies. Those little angles come when they good and ready.

Women can heal a crying child with just a kiss on a scar, women can make a full course meal out of scraps, women can fight battles with just her words, women stand strong again and again after every beat down, she can wipe away the hardest man's tears just by rubbing his back, and she came move mountains with just one look. Some women can make wars, and some can end wars, it's all in how she plays the game. Now, we do have some woman that are not capable to do any of these things only because they choose not to, or they never had the opportunity to get shown how to stand strong as a woman. But I do believe God gave us that extra little gift that men just don't have. I don't know what it is called or how to explain it, but we have it. Now, we do have some women who don't have sense God gave a gnat's ass but they still learning. That would be a whole other conversation."

I guess you are wondering why I brought all of that up and I don't have any children? Well, I don't have to have children to know how powerful a woman can be. I see it in my clients at the firm and at the grocery store, I watched a woman make a full dinner for her family with just $10. What about the grandmother taking care of six grandchildren while the parents work two jobs to make ends meet? Power is all in how you handle your struggles, knowing that no matter what, you will come out on top. It's all about choices, God gave us all free will and the opportunity to make the right choices, even when we choose the wrong ones. He will let you fall and get back up to dust yourself off to try it again, and that what makes Him so wonderful."

As I wrote down her words, I noticed she got silent again. I wondered to myself, "Why does all of the women I have interviewed do that? I know they are reflecting on things from their past, but it seems like they all do it at the same time. They'll get started, then they stop.

"Kris?" she said, "Things are not always what it seems. For example, I'm a lawyer, right? I hear stories and testimonies about the most outrageous things, and I must determine is my client telling the truth, or are they lying. You dig and dig to prove their case or defend them and when the truth comes out, it leaves a courtroom speechless. That's what I think your book is going to do, leave some people speechless. I don't know all the other women stories, but I have one that just might make you scratch your head.

About eleven years ago, my sister and I were going to the mall to buy our father a gift for Father's Day when we decided to stop at a gas station to grab some bottle water. While we were at the gas station, Mercy and I noticed a young lady around eighteen years of age or so that was standing at the end of the store, she was just standing there looking around with a strange look on her face like she was lost. I glanced at her for a minute then walked into the store. Mercy, on the other hand, got ready to walk over there to her to make sure she was safe and if she needed anything. Mercy has always been the type of person that lived on the edge, she was not afraid of nothing and nobody on this earth. My auntie told her one day that if she ever got kidnapped, the kidnappers would bring her tail back because she would probably talk their heads off or pull out some type of gun out of her weave. My sister is a force to be reckoned with, that girl has a side to her that would scare the roughest person in prison.

Anyway, she went over to talk to the young lady to see what was going on with her. I told Mercy that she doesn't know if it's a set up to get robbed or not. Maybe the young lady is waiting on a ride or whomever she is with is inside the store. Mercy doesn't care, she will face a bullet if she had too.

Mercy walked over to the young lady and started talking to her as I walked into the store. The whole time, I never took my eyes off her. I grabbed two waters and walked over to the checkout counter. As I was standing there, I saw Mercy give her some money and pointed to my SUV. The young lady smiled and shook her head and began to walk into the store. As she came in, I started to walk pass her and that's when she gave me a strange look, then she turned and looked over her shoulder to look at Mercy outside with an amazed look on her face. As I walked pass her, I smiled and said, "You're not crazy, that's my twin sister." The girl smiled and said, "Oh okay, I really thought I was losing my mind for a minute. My name is Tracey, she told me to come in and grab me something to eat and she was going to take me to the airport. I hope that is okay with you?" I said, "We will be glad to take you to the airport. We'll be waiting for you in the black BMW outside on pump seven. Take your time darling."

She smiled and continued to shop in the store. I went out the door and walked over to my truck while Mercy stood patiently waiting outside for Tracey. I got in the car and rolled the window down to ask Mercy a question. "Hey woman, what the hell are you doing? We don't know that girl from a whole it the ground, she could be a set up person to follow us and get robbed, or she could be the robber! What were you thinking?" Mercy looked over at me and said, "Trust God, isn't that what you always say? So, do it. Anyway, I know her. I had her family as a client before. Her father was abusing her and her family, her mom filed for divorce and they just been struggling ever since. Let me handle this and you just be the getaway driver because I sent her in there to rob the store. Just drive when I say go."

I was shocked Mrs. Kris! What has my sister done? What in the hell did she just get me involved in? I was livid! I started yelling at Mercy and asking her what she was thinking and how could she tell that girl that! I took the keys out of the ignition switch and began to walk towards the store. Just when I got in front of my truck, that's when Mercy yelled out, "Girl! Get your paranoid self-back in the truck! I didn't tell that girl that! What type of person you think I am? Oh, ye of little faith looking self! Chill! It was a joke! Gosh! I sent her in there to get her something to eat before we take her to the airport."

She laughed and said, "I feel sorry for your children, you will have them so bound that they will never experience life because your butt will have them on lock down all their lives, live a little. You know I am not going to put us in harm's way! Gee wiz! And you say I need Jesus."

Then my sister had the nerve to roll her eyes at me Mrs. Kris! That woman dances with the devil, I swear she does.

Once Tracey came out of the store, Mercy opened the back door to let her in. She was a pretty lady, she had on some biker jeans with the holes in them with a yellow flowered t-shirt that read, "Unfavorable But Savable" written on the front and on the back of the shirt, it had a cross with a crown on it that was dripping blood on a woman kneeling next to the cross. I thought that was a very unusual shirt, but I loved it. She had on white tennis shoes with yellow and white socks with a yellow ball sticking out of it. One shoestring was white and the other one was yellow. Her hair was braided and pulled up into a bun on the top of her head with a yellow small flower headband. As I can tell, she was a fashionable young lady, she really didn't look like she needed anything. But, like I said before, everything is not what it seems.

Mercy closed the door and I started the truck then we pulled off. No one said anything for about five or ten minutes which made the ride feel very awkward. I put it on the 80's channel because I believe that everyone on this earth has heard an 80's song at least once in their life so that would hopefully break the ice.

Once we got to the first stop light, I looked over and asked Mercy where were we going so I could put it in the GPS system. I looked up at the review mirror and Tracey was looking at me with a strange expression on her face, then glanced back out the window. Mercy turned to me and said, "We are going to take her to 1777 E. Wilmore St, it's off of Pointer and Keller street, by Christ Deliverance Church where Lilly use to stay when we were in college."

It took a minute for me to remember who Lilly was and where she stayed. I shrugged my shoulders and put the address in the GPS, and we were on our way. Tracey didn't say too much in the backseat, so I decided to start the conversation myself. I turned the music down a bit and looked up in the review mirror. "So, Tracey, are you okay? I am very pleased to help you and hope we can do all we can to get you to your destination. Mercy mentioned to me that we are taking you to the airport, but we are in process of taking you to a house. Do you need to grab your things?"

Tracey looked up to the mirror with that same look on her face and said, "Yes, Ma'am. I have a bag already packed. I was trying to get money to catch the bus to South Carolina where my grandmother stays but no one would help me. I have been standing outside of that gas station for about four hours before you pulled up and all I was able to get was $20 in change and a few $1 bills. People are so afraid to help those in need now a days because of the high crime rate.

Nobody helps those in need any more like they used to. There is no telling how long I would have been standing out there if you didn't pull up. Thank You."

I looked at her and said, "You're right about that. Everyone thinks they are going to get robbed or kidnapped so people don't help people anymore, and that's sad. We all need to learn to be kind to one another and maybe the world wouldn't be so dangerous."

Tracey looked over at my in the mirror and said, "Your right, a church bus pulled up for gas this morning with a van full of people, it had to have been 20 or 30 people on that bus. I guess they were going to church or had some type of outing because they were singing praises in the van. Out of that entire church van, two people came up to me to see was I okay. One offered prayer and the other person gave me $2, then walked off. I heard one older lady say, "Lord Jesus, show her grace and mercy."

Tracey paused for a minute then let out silent laugh then said, "And they want to know why folks don't go to church anymore. Just a bunch of fake Christians." Once she said that, I heard Mercy laugh too. I looked over at her with my right eyebrow raised and said, "What's funny?"

Lord I knew that question was about to spark a debate in the car and to this day, I wish I never said that. Mercy stopped what she was doing in her phone and said, with an evil smile on her face,

"Grace, you out of all people should know where this conversation is about to go. As usual, you start it and I am going to finish it. Let me explain what Tracey is talking about. First, she stood outside for four hours and all she was able to get was $20. Four hours! She said that church bus pulled up that morning and only two people got out to see if she was okay. Two people! Out of almost 30 people on that bus! TWO! One offered her prayer, and the other gave her $2! What kind of church is this number one? And two, why isn't she already on her way to South Carolina?! The bus ticket is only $98 to begin with! You mean to tell me, a van full of holier than thou Christians couldn't make sure that this young lady was safe and had enough to get here to where she needs to be?! Really?! 30 people on that bus and only two came to see about her! They should have put a prayer circle around her and prayed for her! God said, "When two or three gather in My name, there I am with you.", or something like that, it's in one of those chapters. It was almost 30 of those people! 30! A van full of folks and only two got out! One prayed and the other gave her $2. Why didn't everyone in that van give her something if they supposed to be a church? Who they praying too? What god are they following because maybe I need to put him on trial. The only one I agreed with was the old lady when she said, "Lord Jesus, show her grace and mercy." See, those old souls know how to find Jesus with just words. And she was right, Jesus sent her mercy, now we are going to show her what Grace and Mercy look like and pay to get this woman on an airplane so she can fly to South Carolina. No bus, no begging, no more asking strangers can they help her, nothing! God showed her Grace and Mercy, that is all she needs to get by until she gets on her feet.

That just turns my gears when folks do that. And the world wants to know why people are turning away from God. That's because they don't know how to be real Christians anymore. They act one way at church for two hours out of the week and the rest of the week they all over the place. But then have the nerve to look down on others for their life situations. I love God, I worship Him daily, hourly, and every second of my life, but just because I'm not kicking and screaming all in church, singing every word that comes out of my mouth, I like to hear different songs besides church music on the radio all day, and drink my brandy on the weekends or after a major case in court, that makes me less than a Christian? Slap yourself! Jesus took and used the ones that wasn't living a good life and made them into followers, but folks don't see that part. And you Grace, you walked right past her, you didn't ask me if we needed anything or if she was okay or nothing. What does that say about you?"

I looked at her with amazement and said, "You told me to go get water and you went to talk to her! You didn't give me time to say anything to her because you had already sent her into the store for some stuff! And then she was walking to the car! Girl don't come for me! I look just like you and no one will notice you are missing!" I turned back around and kept driving.

Mercy rolled her eyes and said, "Ugh! I'm done talking because this isn't about me, it's about Tracey. She turned to Tracey and said, "My bad bruh!"

"After that long rant, Mercy turned and started looking out the window. I was stunned Mrs. Kris, that was the true meaning of open a can of whoop A... because she always expressed how she truly feels about certain things. I decided not to ask her how she felt about the other customers who came to the store and just gave her change. I didn't need to hear anything else from her or we would be arguing about this all night until she wins her case.

Let's take a break Mrs. Kris so you can give your hands a break. Maybe you should get you a bigger tape recorder for your next interviews, I think that would be easier." As she got up, I put my pen down and said, "Your right, I was so excited to get this book rolling, I didn't have time to go buy one. I will put that on my to do list."

I put my pen and paper down, popped my knuckles and stood up for a big stretch. I walked around the living room for a minute to put the circulation back in my legs because I felt stiff for a moment. While I was walking, I stood there and wondered what was going on with Tracey and why she was leaving, or was she running away. Mercy said she represented her before with her mother in a domestic violence case with her farther. I know Grace can't tell me what happened with that case for legal purposes but maybe her comment about her seeing the face of God is attached to this story, only time will tell.

I sat back down and began to google tape recorders while I waited on Grace to come back. As I looked around the room, pictures of the family warmed my heart and made me think of my family and how much I love them. I noticed one picture with a man and a woman sitting at a dining table or some sort, it might have been a fancy restaurant or something. I got up to get a closer look at the picture and noticed that the woman in the picture looks just like Grace. I thought to myself that this must be her mom and dad because the woman was pregnant in the photograph. As I glanced harder at the picture, I noticed a woman in the background with an uneasy look on her face sitting three tables behind them. Maybe she was upset about something and it was caught on film. Oh well, it was a very beautiful photo anyway. I went to sit back down to wait for Grace and that's when her phone rang.

"Mrs. Kris! Can you grab that for me, I'm in the restroom, I'll be right out! Grace yelled. "Sure! I said and reached for the phone.

"Hello, Ms. Givens residents." Silence, so I said hello again. "Hello? Givens residents." The person on the other end was silent for a minute and then spoke. "Hello? Am I calling the right person? I'm looking for Grace."

I replied, "Yes, this is Ms. Givens phone, she stepped away for a second and she wanted me to catch the phone for her. May I ask who's calling?" The lady on the other end laughed and said, "Oh yes, this is Tracey, I was just calling to check on her and to see what she was doing. Is she there?" Total shock went over my body as I held the phone. This is really Tracey, the young lady that Grace was talking about, I was amazed. I calmed down and shuck myself out of total shock and said, "Yes ma'am she's her, I'll go get her for you, just a second." Before I could lay the phone down, I heard her say, "Ma'am? May I ask you your name?" I laughed and said, "Sure! My name is

Kris, I'm a friend of Grace's and we are just here having girl time. Every woman needs a release to chat, gossip, and sip on some lemonade you know." Tracey said in a worried tone, "Your right, especially Grace, she really needs to release some stuff. Well, let her know I'm on the phone will you, I won't take up too much of your girl's day activities. Thanks."

Okay, due to the fact that I am writing a book, I was not intitled to tell her what I really was there for, so I made up the hanging out thing. No woman is to be identified in my book, so I played it off. But I wondered why she said that Grace needs to release some things in the tone she said it in. Oh well. I told her to hold on and I was going to go get Grace, so I put the phone down and yelled out her name, "Grace! Tracey is on the phone!" as I said that, I turned around and Grace was standing right behind me.

Now me being the person that I am, and me knowing that I watch too many movies, the first thing that popped in my head was to swing my fist and punch whoever was up on me. I've seen those same scary movies that everyone else has seen when that creepy person came out of nowhere and then murders everyone. Sneaking all up behind folks and stuff. We don't do that where I'm from, it will not end well for the person sneaking up behind folks. That only happens in the movies and usually those people don't live tothe end of the movie. This ain't no movie. Yes, I wrote the word AIN'T!

I turned around laughing and said, "Girl, you were about to get knocked out! I didn't hear you walk up." She put her hand on my shoulder and said, "You sound just like Mercy, she always ready to puch somebody. She watches scary movies just so she can be ready for anything. I told you that girl needs Jesus." We both laughed and she walked past me to get the phone. I wanted her to have privacy so I walked outside to my car to get my charger for my phone so I could charge it while I'm here. I walked back into the house and went into the living room and that's when I heard Grace say, "You don't know what you're talking about, you and Angel are really starting to worry my nerves with this mess. Angle will be over here shortly, and I will talk to her when she gets here. I have to go darling; I have company. Goodbye!" before she hung up, I heard Tracey say, "Let me say goodbye to Mrs. Kris first." So, Grace passed me the phone and sat back on the couch. I grabbed the phone and said "Hello?" "Mrs. Kris, nothing is as it seems." Then she hung up. I played it off after she hung up and said, "it was nice taking to you too Tracey, Bye Bye!"

I hung the phone up and sat back onto the couch across from Grace. As she sipped her lemonade, I couldn't help but think should I end this session, or should I go to a public place to finish this. My daughter knows where I am so if I am not back in an appropriate time, I know she will send the squad to come look for me. Also, I am under God's protection so I should just relax and act like Tracey didn't just tell me anything that sounded like a brain teaser. So, I put on my famous poker face and continued my session.

"So, Tracey is the one you were talking about?" she looked at me with a huge smile and said, "Yep. I am so sorry for the interruptions we have been having and I know you have other people you need to go see so let's get started, shall we? Where did we leave off?" I looked over my papers and read back to her the last thing she said, "After that long rant, Mercy turned and started looking out the window." You stated that you two had just picked up Tracey to take her to a house to get her things so you could drop her off at the airport.

"Right" she said. "Now after Mercy went on a ramp page about how people treat each other in a time of need, I continued driving. We finally reached the destination and Tracey jumped out the truck before I could put it in park. Mercy got out right behind her and stood at the end of the porch to wait for her. I looked around the area to see if anything strange was going on or if I can notice anyone. It was a very beautiful neighborhood, everyone kept their yards up, kids playing outside, old grandmothers sitting on the porches with switches in one hand and a broom in the other. I laughed because you don't see that anymore, that's that good old school neighborhood watch right there. We didn't need security back then, all the security we needed was the elders in the hood sitting on the porch or hanging out of the windows watching everything. They didn't have guns and alarm systems. They had a switches, the streetlights, and a telephone to call the other neighbors when they see the kids getting out of hand. Everyone on that street had the right to beat your tail if you got out of line rather you were related to them or not. No one called Child Protective Services or Department of Children Services when a kid got a spanking, all they told were the granddads or the uncles of the neighborhood that always were working on someone's car up the street and that was enough. But this generation rarely has that anymore.

As I looked at Mercy standing by the porch, I heard a loud bang and then seen Tracey slowly walking out of the house. I jumped from the sounds of the bang and started the truck up. I yelled out the window to ask them what that noise was then I heard Mercy yell, "It was nothing but a car backfiring, let's go." I saw Tracey walking from the house with a look of paranoia on her face. Mercy opened the trunk up to put her bags in while Tracey got into the backseat. All I could do was think that noise we heard was not a car backfiring. I glanced around the neighborhood and didn't see anyone running nor screaming so I didn't let it bother me anymore. I turned to Tracey in the backseat and asked her was she alright and if she got what she needed, but she didn't speak a word. Mercy looked at me and said, "Drive, she's fine."

The ride to the airport was a quite one. Nothing but the radio was playing the sweet sounds of the 80's music. Mercy reached over and changed the radio and said, "No wonder your twisted Grace, you know there are other music genres out here that sounds just as good, right? Put on some R&B or some hip hop, you're not going to burn in hell if you listen to a little upbeat, up to date songs woman." I didn't say anything, I just let her change the radio.

We finally made it to the airport where we would be dropping Tracey off at. I parked the truck so we could go in and pay for her ticket to South Carolina and to give her a check for $2,000 to get one her feet and to find a hotel to stay in for the moment.

"Grace!?" Mercy said, "do you think $2,000 would sustain her? That might last her a week and a half. The hotels there are pricey, and she is not staying in a whole in the wall rat infested hotel." I looked at Mercy with irritation on my face and said, "Well how much will she need Mercy? We already paying $550 for a first-class seat to get there." Mercy turned to me and said, "If we have it, bless someone with it. That's what I live by, what other ideas do you have? Are you a full woman of God or the woman of God that was on that bus who gave her $2 when she had $500 in her purse?" I looked at her in amazement and said, "How do you know how much that lady had in her purse Mercy? Are you a psychic now?" Mercy opened her purse and took out her check book and said, "No, and I don't want to be, but I'm not stupid either! That church bus just came from Las Vegas! And I know damn well they were not at a church conference because the guy that prayed for her said he didn't have any money to give her because he had lost it all in Vegas! How many times do I have to tell you, nothing is as it seems? Wake up Grace! Go pay for the ticket, I'm going to give her a check for $3,000, that will give her $5,000 to get on her feet until she finds a job and a place to stay. Never mind that, I'm going to give her $5,000, that will make her have $7,000 to take with her. That's enough to do all that and maybe a deposit on an apartment or something. But dad named you Grace!" she said with an attitude. "No wonder he named me Mercy because I am the only one that always shows mercy to those in need. I'll be back, I'm going to take out $500 out of the ATM so she can have cash on her when she lands."

Mercy walked off mummering something under her breath with a frown on her face. Tracey stood off on the side like she was embarrassed to be seen with us because we were arguing in the middle of the airport. When I returned with the ticket, I noticed that I didn't see Mercy anywhere. I asked Tracey did she see where my sister went, and she said that she was waiting for me in the truck. I thought that was odd because Mercy is the one who knows Tracey very well, not me. Anyway, I gave Tracey the plane ticket and gave her a big hug. She turned to me and said, Ms. Grace, I really appreciate what you did for me, I will forever be grateful to you. I wish I could tell you everything that has gone on but in due time, everything will reveal itself to you. I will call you both when I land and when I am settled into a hotel. I will keep in touch with you as much as possible if you don't mind, thank you for everything." Tracey reached up and gave me a hug, then said, "I'll call you tonight, thanks again."

Tracey walked off towards her gate entrance and looked back and waved again at me. I waved back at her then turned to go back to my vehicle. I reached into my purse to find my keys and then realized, I never gave Tracey my number, how was she going to be able to call me? After racking my brain about it, I finally made it to the car. Mercy was walking up at that time and asked me how I was doing. "Mercy, I have a question, Tracey said she was going to call me tonight once she got settled but I never gave her my number."

"Grace, I gave her our business cards when I gave her the cash out of the ATM machine. Why are you even questioning this? That girl will be ok, chillout." I looked at Mercy and wondered what her story was, so I decided to ask. "Mercy, what happened to her? We both are lawyers so you can tell me why we just gave this young lady $7,500 to get on her feet. We don't treat all of our clients like this, so why her?"

Mercy looked at me with a confused look on her face and said, "Do you remember a case that I was on when I use to come home stressed and in tears all the time? I was on a domestic violent case that was out of the ordinary. The father beat the mother all the time. He would tie her up to the bathroom sink and beat her till she was unconscious, made the kids eat out of the garbage, kick the mother in the stomach after intercourse and make the kids eat his own feces and tell them it was Swedish meatballs. He would put seasoning on it to hide the smell and he would make the mother drink his urine and told her it was lemonade. He was the devil reincarnated. He never did one day in jail because the mother refused to press charges because she thought he would kill her children. Instead, she divorced him, got put in protected custody and they girls went and stayed with their Auntie Bella something, she had a weird long name. Anyway, the mother went through torment in that marriage, the unspeakable acts that she endured would turn anyone insane. It takes a strong woman to get through something like that. Months and months of having to get beaten just because she said good morning, spit in her face after he smoked a pipe, he would invite his friends over and get them drunk and have sex with his wife then beat her for having sex with other men. He would think of unthinkable acts just to have a reason to abuse her. He would lock the kids in the basement for days at a time and made them watch while he tortured their mother. How can a young girl at the age of seven handle trauma like that? What kind of monster God let's walk the face of the earth like that? Demons walk the earth too and they come in all shapes and forms. Love everyone, but trust no one."

I sat back on the couch and glanced at Grace with tears in my eyes wondering what kind of inhumane person could do this to a someone. I did a story a month ago on a woman that had that similar thing happen to her. How, and where is God in all of this? Why would God allow this torturous thing to contiue? The only feeling I had was rage. Even though I didn't know this family or Tracey, I would have been beside myself with anger and revenge.

"Grace?" I said with tears rolling down my face, "What did you feel after Mercy told you all of this? What went through your mind after hearing all of that?"

Grace look over and said, "That's why I am a lawyer, I feel sadden by Tracey story but if I took home all of the pain and suffering from each client I represented, then I would be locked up in a loony bin somewhere. We lawyers must learn how to separate ourselves from the case every time we go home. Yes, it's painful, yes, it's sad and uncomfortable but in the end, we try and make things better by helping clients close a chapter in their lives. Every bit count's, rather it be winning or losing, we made a difference in someone's life. But for some reason, Mercy wanted to help Tracey more than she has helped anyone else."

As I looked upon Grace's face, I realized that she was really concerned about why Mercy helped that young lady out, so I decided to ask her.

"Grace? Can you tell me a little more about Tracey? What is she doing now and is she happy in South Carolina?"

Grace looked up from her cup and sat it down on the table and started to speak. "Well, Tracey is a Therapist now for the mentally ill here in Indianapolis, she moved back here about two years ago to be closer to Mercy and I. She moved to South Carolina to be with her grandparents so they could help her get back to herself and they put her through college to get her master's degree in Psychology. Whatever made her do that, I couldn't tell you. I believe she was in school for almost eight years or maybe ten, I can't remember. Once she graduated, Mercy said she moved back here to Indianapolis to be closer to her. Her plans were to pay us back for helping her change her life. She is currently helping her mom and other siblings with counseling and making sure they were ok mentally and financially stable. She comes by here to see Mercy and I at least twice a week. Her Auntie Bella lives about six blocks from here and we are very close.

Do you remember when I told you that we took her to a house to get her things before we took her to the airport? Well, about a week later after she had left, Mercy told me that she had to go to a funeral for someone she knew a long time ago. Well, that funeral was the funeral of Tracey's friend father, Chuck Tucker who served time in jail years ago. He changed his name to Chuck after he was released. I know how this may sound Mrs. Kris, but Tracey is a very smart girl. I will need you to write down exactly what I am about to tell you so your readers can put things together."

Once Grace said that, I began to have a puzzled look on my face, the first thing that came to my mind was two words, "Oh Sh..." I sat up in my seat and readjusted myself so I can get ready to write whatever she was about to tell me because this must be interesting if she told me to write down word for word what she is about to say. I wondered to myself, would this even be able to be printed for this type of book? What will my readers think if this is about to turn into a totally different chapter than from the rest of my testimonies? I looked at her and told her, "Grace, if what you are about to say goes against the purpose for this book, I will get it edited to where it can flow along with the rest of the book. Any foul profanity will not be printed, I will write it down but would fix some of your words so it can meet my approval. I just wanted to tell you that before you continued. Will that be okay with you?" Grace took a deep breath and said, "Whatever you need to do Kris, just please put it in your book." We both agreed and we continued.

"Now the day we took Tracey to this house to get her things, it wasn't until a week later when Mercy told me whose house it was. Mercy told me since the state put Tracey's family in protective custody, everyone names got changed to protect their identity. Well, while Tracey grew up and all the moving around they did, she ended up meeting a girl name Pam Jenkins and they became best friends. Tracey spent a lot of time with Pam after school and on weekends so she could have a friend to talk to when she had breakdowns or just to have positive people to be around her. Now Pam had a mother named Janet who was married to a man named Chuck and they had three children together. Pam loved having Tracey with her because she had two brothers and she always wanted a sister. They both were the same age; they took all their classes together and had a home life that Tracey felt she always wanted. Tracey spent more time over there with Pam more than she did at home with her mom. Pam's dad worked on an offshore oil rig, so he was barely home at times. When he did come home, they all went out on outings and even took Tracey with them on a trip to the Bahamas for a week on spring break. It was a life that Tracey adored. Well, something happened between the time we picked up Tracey and the week before that.

All that time her and Pam spent together was a plan from the beginning. You see, Pam's father was Charles from the beginning and Tracey knew exactly who he was when she first saw him. She never once mentioned it to Pam, nor her mother. Yes, Pam was Tracey's half-sister. How you may ask, well let me explain. When Tracey and her family got taken away into protective custody, they had their names changed and relocated multiple times. After Charles spent time in jail, he got out for some odd reason and that man carried on with his life like nothing ever happened. He got remarried and had three children, a girl and two boys. His wife worked for a detective agency and he got a job on the oil rig. I heard he found Jesus and repented for his past life, Whatever.

Anyway, he apparently got his life together and moved towards God more because he was a deacon at his church and his wife was the youth choir director. Weird, isn't it? A man like that giving his life over to Christ after he did what he did to Tracey and her family. How and why would God forgive him for the tortuous things he did to them? God has, and will always be a mystery to me when it comes to forgiveness.

While Tracey spent many days with Pam and her family, never once did Tracey mention what happened and what her family went through. She told Pam she needed support as a friend because of how their family was living and loved to come to her house so her mom could have personal time with her friends. Never once, for years, did Tracey let herself be known. As Mercy put it, it was a plan from the beginning. When Tracey had a breakdown and nightmares of what happened to her, she played it off and said she was struggling to be accepted by friends and stressing about college. College, Right.

The reason why Tracey was at the gas station that day was because Charles had given her a check to pay for all four years of college and bought her and Pam a car so they could get around and be roommates. That's when Tracey had the meltdown and ran out the house. She used her last few dollars to call her mother to tell her she was sorry for what she did, and to call her grandparents to ask could she come stay with them. Her mom was looking for her the whole time after that phone call. Her grandparents called her mom and said that Tracey was coming to stay with them for a while and she need not worry. Tracey had planned this the whole time. Now when we picked her up and took her to the house to get her clothes, she stayed in there for about 20 or 25 minutes or so before we heard the bang. Kris? I found out a week later that it was not a car backfiring, they were gunshots like I thought, and Mercy knew it. Chuck had killed himself in the living room right before Tracey walked out of the door. That explained why she had that look on her face when she came out.

Tracey felt anger, rage, and vengeance when Chuck gave her those gifts to her and Pam. She said the love he showed her and the acceptance of her being a part of their family took over her mind and thoughts of killing him ran through her soul constantly. But she had a future to begin and she wasn't going to mess that up for anyone, not even for the devil himself. She thought, "How could this bastard give this family the world and he gave us hell on earth? How could this man love this family but hated us? How could this beast give Pam what she wanted and all I wanted was a happy family and a father, but instead we got a beast? How could this man give himself over to Christ and I can't have children to give my own husband when I get married because of him? Where was God in all of this? She hated God, the day she met Pam's family, period. She assumed Chuck didn't treat that family like that because Pam's mom was a cop and she always was strapped. If he even thought about messing with them, he would have died on the spot.

When Tracey went into the house to get her things, Mercy told me that she had packed the night before and told Pam she was moving back in with her mom until college began. Pam and her mom had gone to the college to get all the paperwork in order so they could move in the following month which left Chuck home alone. When Tracey entered the home, she said Chuck was sitting on the couch watching a movie with a beer in one hand and a sub sandwich in the other. Tracey came into the house and spoke then went upstairs to gather her things. Once she went downstairs, Chuck was still sitting in front of the TV. Next to him was Pam's mothers' gun and badge she left at home. Tracey glanced over at the gun and I believe for a second, thoughts of pulling the trigger, but didn't. Mercy said Tracey walked over to him and grabbed the remote and turned the TV off. He looked up in amazement and asked her what she was doing, and did she need to talk about anything. Tracey threw the remote on the floor and pulled out an old picture of them when he was married to her mom and shoved it in his face. He jumped back and held the picture in his hand, looked up at Tracey and said, "The whole time? But your name is Tracey, how, when?" Tracey looked at him and said,

"Father, our names got changed in protective custody to keep you away from us. I was young then dad, now I'm all grown up, you didn't recognize your own daughter. Oh, wait, you couldn't because of all the times you disfigured our faces! I have been in your house with you for years and you didn't even know it was me. I've watched you carefully father, you gave this family the life you were supposed to have given us! but all we got was pure hell from you and now you call yourself a Christian! You are not even worthy of God's love and I will make sure you relive those days of torture in your head from this day forward. I told Pam everything and right now they are not coming back. They did not leave to get our dorm room ready for us to move, they are with my mother right now listening to everything you've ever done to us and showing your perfect little family all the scars you've given us. I hope you rot in the pits of hell for the rest of your life, and when you die of old age and go to hell, I will be there waiting for you, seated right next to the devil himself, you sick and evil bastard."

She glanced at Chuck with a huge evil smile on her face, looked down at his food and said, did you enjoy your beer and meatball sub dad? I added a few of my personal ingredients just for you! And wash it down with the special beer I got for you and placed it in the refrigerator, you dirty, evil, son of a ....! Rot in hell dad, oh yeah, and mom says hi."

Trace left Chuck speechless and crying in the living room, by the time she got to the fourth step on the porch, that's when we heard a loud bang. Chuck had killed himself in the living room.

"Kris?" Grace said, "Pam and her mom was not at Tracey's mothers house, they were actually at the college getting things together. They knew nothing about Tracey and what she went through as a child. It was all a plan to get back at her father, but Tracey had no idea that her father was going to kill himself. That was not in her plans, her plan was to try and make him remember what he had done to her family and let him know that her mother had overcome the mental, physical, and emotional abuse he bestowed upon them."

After I heard that story, I couldn't even look at Grace. I was staring off into the daylight because of what I just heard. The only thing I thought of was the beer and sub sandwich. I shuck myself out of a trance and said, "Um, Grace, did Tracey really give that man that sandwich like that with that beer? Grace laughed and said, Nope, He was so messed up in the head by what she said to him, he had forgotten that he had bought the sandwich and beer himself at the deli up the street from his home. Isn't it amazing how words can kill you quicker than a gun can? God said, "Life and death is in the power of the tongue" I guess Tracey knew that. She played on what she knew about the power of the tongue, and it worked. She had mentioned to Mercy that every time he came home off the oilrig, he would always go to the deli and get a meatball sub and beers to watch old movies all night. I guess he forgot that too, and Tracey worked everything into her plans perfectly. When she found out the next day after talking to Pam, that's when she felt bad about what she done and decided to tell Pam that she wasn't coming back, she had told her she left to go stay with her grandparents. Anything after that I don't know because Mercy never mentioned anything else to me about it. Tracey is a therapist now and I never brought any of that stuff back up again."

As I sat there in amazement, I finished writing what just took place and I closed my book for now. I had to shake it off, so I told her I wanted to go on the porch to call my husband to check on him. While I was on the porch, I noticed a black Lexus pull up and a woman got out. She was dressed very professionally like a doctor or something. She had on a black pencil skirt, black stockings, black heels and a white blouse with ruffles hanging in the front of the shirt. As she approached the steps, I put my phone down and moved to the side to get out of the way of the door. She reached her hand out to me and said, "Hi! you must be Mrs. Kris? Nice to meet you, my name is Angle Givens, Graces' Auntie, nice to finally meet you." I looked in amazement and said, "Oh Hi! I've heard so much about you. She's in the house right now, I was taking a breather to call and check on my family because I've been here for a while and I wanted to let him know I was okay and that I was still visiting Grace." She smiled and said, "Oh that's okay, take your time, I'll be in here talking to Grace. Has she been talkative today?" I said, "Yes, very, but it's okay, I enjoy her company. She mentioned you were coming, and that Mercy would come over to meet me as well, also Tracey." Right when I said that, a white Benz pulled up and a young lady dressed in a yellow and white pants suit got out of the car. As she walked up the drive, Angel said, "Speak of the devil." Then walked into the house. I thought, how ironic she would say that after I heard what I just heard.

Soon as she got close to the house, I remembered that I left all the papers on Grace's coffee table and that I had to rush and hide them before they saw it. Tracey walked up to me and said, "Hello Mrs. Kris, nice to see you still here. Come on in." When she said that, I immediately shock her hand and raced back into the house to gather up all my paperwork before any of them seen it. Luckily, they were standing in the kitchen with Grace laughing and talking. As they talked in the kitchen, I grabbed the papers and stuck them in my briefcase. Once I closed the briefcase, I joined them in the kitchen. When I walked in, I saw Grace's smile go away then she walked away into the living room. I guess she thought I left the work out on the table and she wanted to go check and see. I looked at her and nodded my head to let her know it was put away and then she started smiling again.

Tracey walked over to me and said, "So Mrs. Kris, how's it going? Everything ok?" I looked at her and said, "Yeah, things are great, just having girl time." Tracey walked with me in the hallway and I decided to ask her about the pictures. Before I could ask her, Angle walked up and said, "Ladies, let's go into the living room and sit down. Mrs. Kris, we are going to go to dinner, would you like to come? My treat."

"Sure, I said, just let me call my husband and let him know I'm okay and that I will be going with you all to dinner. Thanks for the invite, the more the merrier. Will Mercy be joining us as well, Grace told me she was coming?" Tracey looked at me and said, "Yes, she'll be there too." As we went into the living room, I asked Angel about all the pictures in the hallway and if she could tell me which one was Mercy, and which one was Grace because she had mentioned that Angel was the only one who could tell them apart. I looked over my shoulder and seen Grace go upstairs while saying, "I'll be back ladies, I'm going to go change clothes real quick and freshen up, be back shortly." We all yelled, "Okay!" I stood there looking at the pictures and Angle came up on one side and Tracey on the other side of me. Angel glanced at all the pictures and said, "Man, it's a lot of memories on this wall, we've been through a lot in this family, but God made sure we could get through it together as a family." Tracey looked at Angel and said, "Amen to that sister." I kept looking over all the pictures and Angle was laughing and saying things like, I remember that, and I remember this. So, I decided to ask her who was who.

"Angle, I've heard so much about Mercy, which one is she? They look so much alike." Angle smiled and said this one is Mercy, the picture with her standing next to her father. She was mad that day because her dad caught more fish than she did. Look at his one, she was mad in this picture because I took her picture off guard, she hates that." Once she said that, Tracey said, "Angle, enough, quit playing." Angle looked over at her and said, stay out of grown folks' business." Then laughed.

"Mrs. Kris, Mercy is in all of these, so is Grace. Look harder, all the pictures with one smiling and one frowning all the time, you can tell the difference in who is who. Grace is always happy and bubbly, and Mercy is always mad and frustrated about something.

Mrs. Kris." Angle said, "Grace and Mercy are the same person."

My world stopped in an instance. My heart fell out of my chest, I couldn't breathe, I started coughing, sweating, my legs got weak and my blood pressure shot through the roof! My mouth fell open and my eyes wider. What on earth have I gotten myself into? Who in the world was I in the house with? The first thing that came to my mind was LEAVE! This whole family is bat crazy! Dear Jesus, what on earth are you doing to me?! Dear God! I got to go!! Book canceled! Throw the whole book away! Burn everything! Words were popping in my head that I dare not to write. The whole time this woman was talking about herself! Jesus help me!

"WHAT!?" I yelled; you mean the whole time it was never a Mercy Givens? Who have I been talking too for four hours? Dear God, I'm about to pass out." Tracey went into the kitchen to get me a cup of water while Angle sat me down in a chair at the bar. "So, is she really a lawyer? Who and where did Mercy come from? What is this woman's real name? Is everything she told me a lie?" Angle laughed and said, "Well, it depends on what you all talked about." I looked at Angle and said, "You all!? How many are they?" Angle laughed and said, "Calm down Mrs. Kris and breath, I know all about why you are here and what you two were doing. Please keep her in your book and write everything she said. Yes, everything she told you was true, I listened to the whole conversation on the camera system we installed last year. What she said about her father was true, what she said about her mother was true, and her being a lawyer was true too, ten years ago. She hasn't practiced in a long time" Tracey walked in and said, "Everything she told you about me was true Kris, everything she said happened, but when she was mad about the things with my father triggered Mercy to take the case. I guess you are thinking what everyone else thinks, how in the world is she a lawyer and who would let her practice as a lawyer with a split personality? Well, Mercy is her inner self, everyone has one. People act one way at certain times and another at other times. She reminisced on when she was a lawyer and a good one at that, but it got worse the older she got so we convinced her to stop practicing. I was her last case. She is perfectly fine. Her real name is Grace Mercy Givens. When her mother died, her father prayed for Grace to survive the delivery. Her father prayed and prayed to God and He showed her father mercy, and Grace lived. So, he named her Grace Mercy Givens. He always called her Grace and Mercy and I believe she took on a whole other identity when bad things happened. Mercy would do and say things that Grace wouldn't. She was the only child and if you look back at everything, she told you and put two and two together, you can tell the parts that sounded strange. Like when she saw me in the store and I looked at her crazy, when she was standing on the porch when my father killed himself, that was Grace with me the whole time. In the airport, I was embarrassed because she was arguing with herself in the middle of the airport. Even though things sounded crazy, she still helped those in need and she, or shall I say, they, are wonderful people."

As I tried to process this information, I was able to calm down from the shock that I was experiencing. I looked at Angle and Tracey and said, "I can't put this in the book, it wouldn't be right. Grace has no idea what she was doing. A friend of hers referred me to her and she asked her if she wanted to be in the book and she agreed. I don't feel comfortable doing this. I can't put her in it. I won't put her in it. I'm sorry."

When I said that, a voice came from behind me and said, "Put my part in your book Mrs. Kris, I am fully aware of what we are doing and why I did it. I would like to be in your book. Not because of my story, but for Tracey as well. Tracey gave me full permission to tell her story because that was a big part of me and that's when I saw the face of God work in my life. I have been getting plenty of help dealing with things and I do know right from wrong. The reason I used Tracey story is to let you see what I went through mentally. If I would have told you about Mercy from the beginning, you wouldn't have understood what I was going through and how God was working on my behalf. Medications and therapy helps' a whole lot with cases like mine. I'm fine, please believe me, I am honored to be in your book. Do you know why? Because I am the imagine of God when he granted me mercy to come into this world and help keep my father from breaking down from heartache and pain of losing his wife and almost his daughter. This is what breakthrough looks like with the help of God, family, and friends to support you every step of the way. Sometimes it's hard to explain but you must believe me, I'm ok. Please don't take me out."

We all sat down for a minute while I soaked all this in. I had so many questions to ask, so many things running through my head and questions about the mind I had for Tracey. I looked at Grace and said, "This was more about Tracey than it was about you, what about you Grace? What got you into this state of mind? Did something traumatic happen to you for this to happen? When I think about it, I would have to get Tracey to sign a consent form too because it was mainly about her story."

"Mrs. Kris, Grace said, so many things have happened in my life that I would probably need your entire book to explain. I choose this particular story to tell you because that one meant the most to me. People who suffer from what I have has to understand that they are not alone, this is about me, how I think, how I operate, and how I handle stress when I don't receive the right help. So, you see, this is really about me and what I had to go through before I got professional help. People with mental issues aren't all crazy, I see it as thinking differently from everyone else. We're God's special people who has an open mind about things and process differently that's all. Just because we are not like the everyday people doesn't make us any different from others. Just because we don't think like them, we are declared insane or crazy which makes some even more uneasy because they are tired of trying to prove to others that they are okay, normal, we just need a little help every now and then. Don't take me out, please show me grace and mercy and keep me in your book, I know someone will get help from this."

Angel and Tracey looked at Grace and walked over to hug her. At that moment, I saw love and support for a woman of God who just wanted a voice in this world. One day she was a successful lawyer and the next, she was Mercy. My heart melted and I thought to myself, if God didn't want her story in here, He wouldn't have pointed me in her direction. That's when I made the decision to keep her part in here.

WHEN I LOOKED AT GRACES' FACE AND SEEN HOW SINCERE SHE was, that's when I truly knew that God can use anyone He pleases to be a vessel for His glory. I changed her chapters title from "Given Grace", to "Grace and Mercy, The Twins" in honor of Grace Mercy Givens. The most unique women I have ever met.

CHAPTER 8
PHOENIX RISEN

P eople say when life gives you lemons, make lemonade, well I say, when life comes your way with lemons, slam the door in its face. I never liked lemonade anyway, too tart. I can come off as rude, bossy, irritating, drama queen, or just Queen. To the ones who know me inside and out, I'm know as Queen, for those of you who do not know me, my name is Phoenix. Why did my parents name me that? Well let's talk about what a Phoenix is, lets break it down and give you the dictionary term for a Phoenix. (*Phoenix, a mythical bird of great beauty fabled to live 500 or 600 years in the Arabian wilderness, to burn itself on a funeral pyre, and to rise from its ashes in the freshness of youth and live another cycle of years: often an emblem of immortality or of reborn idealism of hope.*) (*www.dictionary.com*)

My favorite meaning that I read on dictionary.com was, " *A person or thing that has become renewed or restored after suffering calamity or apparent annihilation.*" Annihilation, I like that, but honestly, God is still working on me, I have what I call seesaw faith, it goes up and it goes down on a daily base. Luckily, I have grown closer to Jesus/God because without Them, I will not be here.

My name is Phoenix H. Risen, and I rose from my ashes in the freshness of youth to live another day.

My life was never like lemonade, more like beer, you drink it for a buzz and great taste but in the end, it will have you running to the bathroom constantly to pee. Your kidneys were flushed out good but depending on how many beers you had, you can wake up with a hangover, drink too much and your skin will smell like beer. I'm not too fond of beer, I just want to put that out there.

When I think about my life and what I been through, I can honestly say, Thank You Jesus! I should have been dead a long time ago. I am a mother and a wife now with three-college degrees, a great job, wonderful children and a few grandkids. Who knew back then that my life could make a total 360 in just a matter of time? Before I knew it, I was nothing like I use to be, but my temper did not change. I'm hardheaded in that area. Plenty of self-help books though.

When I was a young teenager, I had my first child. I thought my mother was going to throw me out when she found out, I didn't know who I was afraid of the most, God or my mother. Either or, I was expecting to see those pearly gates when my friend and I stood in front of her to tell her I was pregnant. Dear God, she's going to knock me into the middle of the universe. So, after I planned my funeral, called all my friends to bid them farewell, made out my will and kissed my puppy named Joey goodbye, my friend and I walked into the living room and told my mother. But, she didn't, the vision of my untimely death that I imagine and the fiery pits of hell I thought she was about to send me too, shocked me. My mother was more concerned about my health and the baby's health more than anything. She got upset because I waited so long to tell her, and I had not gotten any prenatal care. I can honestly say that my mother is amazing. She did get very upset that I was young and pregnant, but she put that to the side until she made sure I was healthy, and the baby was healthy. I owe a lot to my mom because I did not have to drop out of school, and I was able to get a job and go to work to help with bills.

Once I got older, I end up pregnant two more times, that's when all hell broke loose, mom was pisst then. But I held my own, got on better birth control because that pill thing wasn't working out for me. I didn't get pregnant, but I kept forgetting to take the thing. Between school, work and now three kids, I couldn't even remember my own name. Just in case anyone is questioning about my children's father, he was there the whole time. No, I do not have three different baby daddies', my three children have the same father so get that out your heads, just being real and honest. That's why I'm telling my story. Pure honesty sweetheart.

After a few years' past, I became more independent and doing more on my own, to the point I started to think I was grown. Mind you, my mother helped me take care of my kids while I worked and went to school (high school, just in case you were wondering). I started to feel I had some pull in the house because I was working and helping with the bills with my sibling who was older than me and had already graduated from high school. I started hanging out more with friends, I started smoking weed, and drinking vodka and crown. (Note to those who are reading this, never drink clear liquor the same night you drink brown liquor.) BIG MISTAKE! I know I made mistakes before but that one I learned my lesson the next day and never done it again, EVER! I think I throw up my liver or something that morning.

Let me get back to my story. I graduated high school in 97 and I felt that the world was mine, no limits, no rules, no restrictions. I was grown, so I thought. I started hanging out more and having a lot of friends. I stop drinking every time I went out and stopped staying out late, I finally felt like a real woman, a great mom, and a God-fearing person. I think we all felt that way once we get our lives together. I didn't' know this then, but I know this now, that the devil does not take kindly to faithful God followers who stopped living of the world and walking a straight line with the Lord. The devil will attack just as soon as you think your life is going well. He called for backup with me, a young mother of three who has finally gotten her life together. I had put the past behind me and moved on to better myself for my children and my mom. If you never seen the devil before, let me describe to you what he looks like.

He stood maybe 6'3 or 6'5, nice dark creamy brown skin, low bald fade haircut, very muscular well belt gentleman with tattoos in places you can see just enough to make you lose your religion. His voice was deep like a smooth roaring sound of a quite storm in the middle of the night. His cologne smelled like Love Potion #6, the cologne smelt so good, every time he walked past a woman, her eyes instantly rolled back in her head and will stop to make a double take on what just walked past her. His charming voice made you melt from the inside out and he will make you forget your own name. I won't say his real name, so I'll just call him "Z". Z came into my life when everything was falling into place, I was a single mom now because I chose to be. The kid's dad was still in their life, but I just wanted more out of life. Anyway, I met Z one night at work, he was a customer that came into the store looking for a few things to pick up and he asked me for help looking for something one day. Soon, I started to notice Z was coming into the store at least twice a week and then it went form twice a week to almost every day. After a while, he became a regular customer, we knew regular customers by name so every time he came into the store, my manager would whisper to me, "Your boyfriend is here." I laughed it off and didn't think anything about it.

One day, Z came in and just asked me out on a date. My soul said no but my body said yes! He enchanted me, I fell under his spell and after the fourth date, I was in love. He was the perfect gentleman. Back then, I never let my children see who I dated, I never brought any man around my kids nor my home just in case he was a deranged lunatic then I would have to eliminate him. I learned that from my dear Great Uncle Dylan. We dated for about three or four months and then things began to get weird, I didn't notice it then because I was in love, so I thought. One day he asked me for a favor and that it would benefit us both. Before he told me what it was, I had already agreed to it. He told me that he had a friend who was having a party and one of the strippers didn't show. He told me that all I had to do was dance and that no man at the party could touch me and he would be there with me for my protection. After I thought long and hard about it and realized that my check didn't cover the light bill and I was trying to decide rather to feed the kids or pay the light bill. He told me that I would get $200 just for showing up and all I had to do was give him $80 of that so he could provide good protection for me. Z told me all I had to do was drink a couple of shots to ease my nerves, I never danced before and he assured me that I won't be the only girl there and that it was a private party, no clubs. The only thing I could think about at that time was my children going without lights or food, I had to make a choice, I chose to dance. By the end of the night, I had made $500. That was the quickest $500 I had made in my entire life at that time. I was able to pay the light bill, buy food for the house and give my mom $100 just for her.

I know your saying that's not a lot, but you have to remember, this was the 90's. Now, you got to give the strippers $500 to show up. After that night, I didn't do it again. One day Z and I were talking, and I brought it up and he said that his friend has stopped messing with that business and now he was doing it. Since we were dating, I didn't see nothing wrong with me doing it again just for pocket money, so I stripped more and more. I started hanging out with different friends and left all my real friends alone and I started back drinking and smoking weed. I was hypnotized by the quick cash I was making from a bunch of old men at retirement party's and young unfaithful dudes at bachelor parties that were about to get married the next day. I didn't care, it wasn't me getting married. I started to become a man's real-life fantasy, they thought of it, I became it. I got so wrapped up in it to the point I stop messing with Z and started dating a guy I met at one of the parties. A few girls and I started doing parties that Z didn't even know about and keeping all the money to ourselves. We even started doing lesbian parties. We didn't care because the money was still the same old green paper that we got from the men.

One day I was walking out my house to got to the store and Z pulled up outside. The first thing I thought of was he was coming back to talk so we can get back together. NOPE! He got out the car and began to yell and scream at me because one of the girls went back and told him what we were doing behind his back. We argued for about 20 minutes until my neighbors called the police, then he left. About four months later, he showed up again. Just so happen I had stop stripping and doing private parties and began dating a guy that loved me with my flaws and everything. I was walking out the door one day to get into the car with my boyfriend and I heard loud music coming down the street. I saw a black car on rims came flying down the road with music blasting very loudly. We didn't think nothing of it because folks did that all the time in the hood. This time was different, it was Z.

He seen me get into the car and pull off with my new boyfriend Steven, by the time we made it to the corner of the street, he literally tried to run us over. He drove so close behind the car we were in that if we would have made a sudden stop, we all could have died. My boyfriend drove faster to get him off his tail, in the meantime, while still driving, he called his friends on the phone for them to meet him somewhere because this idiot was trying to kill us. Z was screaming out of his window telling me to get out the car and tried to ram us on the side, before we knew it, he drove faster and had got about five cars in front of us. He stopped in the middle of the street and turned his car sideways on a two-lane street so no one could get pass. Z jumped out the car with a gun aimed at us while walking slowly towards the car. It was a two-lane street and we had nowhere to go. Instantly,

Steven waited until Z got closer to our car and away from his, then, he threw the car in reverse real fast and we got out of there.

I turned around and Z had stopped in the middle of the street and watched us drive off. He ran real fast back to his car and jumped in it. Traffic was backed up now, so it took him a minute to drive through it. We were in the hood, so nobody bothered to call the cops, not even me. I asked Steven to take me home because Z wouldn't think that I would go back there and he said no, then I said I want to go back home just in case he wants to come endanger my kids and I really would go to jail for murder and torture, I would kill that man's entire family.

After a huge argument, he finally took me home. I got out the car and he pulled off. By the time I got to my garage, Z had pulled up and jumped out the car and raced towards me. My kids, my best friend, and her kids were in the house and they had no idea that I was even outside with a man whom I thought was going to kill me, no one even knew.

Z jumped out the car saying that I was his property and that I was a whore for being with another man. He was yelling and belittling me in front of my own house. He grabbed my arms and was shoving me against my car saying he would kill me if it ever happened again. Then for some reason, he started kissing me and grinding on me until a neighbor turned on her side porch light to take the trash out, then Z got quiet. We stood there for a minute and then he got in his car and drove off. I went in the house and told my best friend what just happen, and she said he could have killed me, and they wouldn't have even known. That day, I made up my mind, never again will I ever let a man put his hands on me or even threaten me like that again and I made sure of it. When I was about 4 or 5, I remember seeing my mother get beaten and stomp on like a piece of trash. I refused to even let it get that far with me from that day forth.

As time went on, for some reason, I never seen Z again, nor heard anybody talk about him. I wondered for a split second what he was doing with his life now. A year or so went past and I ran into one of his friends we use to hang with, and he told he got into a real bad car wreck and was hospitalized for a long time. Sorry, but I didn't feel any sympathy for him, not one bit. I asked him where he was living now, and he told me that he was still in the same house taking care of his dad. All I could say was, "Oh really?" with a huge smile on my face.

A few days went by and I decided to pay old Z a visit. I pulled up to his house and knocked on the door. While I waited, I noticed an old man walking towards the door. Then, I realized, it was Z. He was so helpless trying to walk, still, no sympathy, I felt nothing, pure emptiness. I ended up helping him walk to the restroom, helped him eat, and do a few things for him, so I stayed with for a few hours and checked on him a few days of the week.

The reason I did that is because I had to build up my nerves to forgive him for trying to kill me. God forgave him, why can't I forgive him? A lot of people said I shouldn't have forgiven him, but the thing is, I wanted God to forgive me. Z had opened a lot of ungodly doors that I willingly walked into and stayed in long after he was out of my life. I had to seek forgiveness from God for that because He is the one I would have to answer to in the end. Not man.

I thank God for that part of my life because to this day, I don't take no mess off of no man, not even my husband. I respect my husband as a child of God, he knows my entire story and he still wanted to marry me. WOW!

I dated other guys after my experience with Z and I made it known to each of them that I would shoot them right in the forehead if they crossed me or did anything to my kids. Before I met my husband, I dated a guy for 15 years and I had three kids by him, but we lost one due to a complicated pregnancy. So, we have two together now. We never got married because we were in our 20's and marriage wasn't really a big thing back then. I'm not going to use his real name either so I'm going to call him Jody.

God and the Beast is the reason why I am the way I am now. (I will explain who Beast is later).

Jody taught me the ways of the streets, how to survive and how to hustle. Meaning, work a good job that pays the bills, go to college and pursue my dreams. (So did Beast, he taught me first, but our encounter was cut short).

We argued like normal couples, he called me his wife and I called him my husband. He is a wonderful father to his kids and will go the distance to make sure they eat. We been through hell and back together, but I never once had to feel unsafe with him, ever. I got my temper from him; I will go off at the drop of a dime if something doesn't sit right with me. Jody was always about the business of coming up in life, I respected that about him. The years that we had together was precious to me, still is. Jody and I are married now to other people and our spouse's respect the bond that we have because nobody can take that from us. I love his wife, she is an amazing person, that's my girl! As for my husband, he was handpicked by God just for me.

My story is a common story for a lot of women. God brought me through stripping, being gay for a year because I threw my hands up with men. I dated a gang member (Beast), that also taught me how that respect myself more and take care of my kids, to this day, I thank him for that. He always called me his flaming butterfly because they never see me coming. (that's another story). Right now, in my life, I am very happy. My husband Wayne is amazing, we been together for 8 years now and by the time this book comes out, we should be together for about 10 or so.

God still got me here for a reason, He protected me and let me live the life I lived for a reason. I haven't gotten killed, no diseases, my kids are well, my mom is enjoying her life with grandkids and her great grandkids. My husband and I are extremely happy, I thank God for that. Wayne is my rock, my soul shakes every day that I see him, either from anger or from joy, either way, he knows how to make a woman feel like a Queen even, on her bad days.

My oldest son friend called me Phoenix one day, and that name stuck with me. I was annihilated in my life because of the decisions I made, but I always sprung back up out of the ashes and was reborn again in Jesus Christ.

I can't go into detail about my entire life because if I did, I would have to write my own book and I would call it "Phoenix Rising" because I rose above what the devil meant for bad, God turned it into good. A life lesson that I live by to this day with God's help.

If I was to give advice to women, especially young women, I would say that just because it looks good, smells, good, and taste good, doesn't mean it's for you. The devil comes with beauty and charm, don't be deceived, it's not real. If it's for you, God will make in known to you. There is a difference between Love and Lust, please do not get them confused with a blessing and a curse like I did. If you hard up for money and you don't know rather to feed your kids or pay a bill, trust me, God will provide. If you felt like I did, then you know where I'm coming from. Back then, it was nothing wrong with doing something strange for a piece of change to get by, pay a bill, or feeding your kids. Life happens, we can't avoid it, it's up to you to make it work.

In my mid 30's, I was going through and faze in my life where I felt like God wasn't on my side, like He abandon me and turned away from me. Things that I wanted to do in my life kept backfiring and falling through the cracks. So, I started questioning my belief. Why is God not hearing my cry? Did Jesus not go before God and tell Him I needed help and that I am on the verge of a mental breakdown? Did He get mad at me because I said that I was going to stop doing something and I kept doing it anyway thinking that God would forgive me for it because he is a forgiving God? After all that back and forth faith I had, I eventually decided to hold off on church, reading my bible, and I stop praying for myself and just prayed for others. To me, it seemed like Jesus answered everyone prayers but mine. I could pray for someone and then they will get blessed, I could pray for healing for somebody and soon they got healed, I could pray for jobs and finances for others and they would see resolution and peace. But as for me, I saw nothing but hardship and pain, so why pray for myself if He turned away from me? It felt like God said, "Depart from me, I never knew you!" and I battled with that every day. I want to hear those sweet words from Him, "Well done my good and faithful servant."

Phoenix stopped to take a deep breath and wiped away tears from her face. She had so much pain in her eyes, I couldn't find the words to comfort her. I was getting ready to tell her let's stop the session for today then she smiled and said, "Sorry, I know my story is all over the place and I keep jumping back and forth between my past and my present. I bet once you read this in its entirety, it probably won't make any since at all."

I look at her and said, "Darling, let God use you, somebody out there needs to hear this. You're not doing this for me, you're doing this for you, God put it on your heart to agree to this Phoenix, walk in your blessing, embrace your pain so you can feel a release in your life. It doesn't matter if your story is jumping back and forth, and if things don't make since or not. It's your words and I am going to write them exactly how you say them. It will be someone who will relate to what you're saying. A person that has become renewed or restored after suffering calamity or apparent annihilation, remember? That's you Phoenix." She turned and looked at me with so much sincerity in her heart, she had me shedding a few tears.

"Where was I?... Oh yes, faith. I have what I call "seesaw faith" one minute its up and the next minute its down. I was all over the place, praised Him at 12pm and was mad at Him by dinner time. I called on Jesus only when I needed Him, only when everything I tried to do failed because I was doing it on my own and not with Him. I waited until the chips fail, then I expected Him to put them back together for me and when he didn't, I got mad at Him, so, now I was down to the ground on my seesaw and had no plans of coming back up to finish the game. That's when I decided to quit playing the game all together, I got off the ride and walked completely away. I thought to myself, why hang around with somebody who doesn't want me around or who doesn't have my back if I need a little help? That was how I was feeling about my beliefs in God, so he let me walk away freely. He doesn't mess with free will, remember?

How is it that people can do what they want to do in life and others must suffer like hell just to make it through the day? It's not fair! I know my flaws, I mismanage money. I'm so afraid of working for nothing and not being able to enjoy my money that I worked so hard for that I spend it on things I don't need. Who said I can't have that SUV that I wanted? Who says I can't get that ideal job that I want? Who says I can't be wealthy enough to be able to take care of my family or start my own business and have them all on payroll? Well after much deliberation and counseling to myself and God, I've finally came up with the conclusion that I am the reason why I can't have these things. I am the reason why my credit is like it is. I am the reason why I don't have that ideal job and that wonderful SUV that I want. Not God, not the devil, Me!

I stopped myself from advancing in life and furthering myself in my dreams. Why? because I am going about it all wrong. I don't have to work in anyone's business if I don't want too, I don't have to answer to nobody but God. I ask God for what I want and if He thinks I deserve it, then he will give it to me. He opens doors for us all the time, but we are the ones who make the decision to walk through it, or past it. Some of us just stand there and look at the door debating with ourselves if you should go in or not. Then when we decided to walk past it, we get mad because God didn't answer our prayers. Soon we walk away from Him and take matters into our own hands and that's when it all fails. Some have taken matters into their own hands and it worked out well for them, but only for a moment because God wasn't in it from the jump.

It's like our kids, we tell them to live right, clean they rooms, respect each other and do your homework. Instead, they keep they room dirty, hide the homework, disrespectful to others and always glued to their phones or the computers on social media, adults too. So like God, us as parents, we must take things away from them just to teach them a lesson. Kids get upset and they hate life and don't want to be in the house anymore and run tell they friends and siblings that they hate their parents. They say, we don't have homework! or We already done it at school! lying the whole time. Hmmm... sounds familiar doesn't it?

We act like kids when God take things away from us when we do wrong or if our attention gets distracted for too long. We stop going to church, we stop talking to Him, we tell everyone why God isn't real. We even stop doing our own homework ourselves (reading the bible). When that happened to me, I instantly realized that He is trying to get my attention! Praise God! I don't know if that statement was coming from my thoughts or from Him? I could never tell the difference.

My mom used to tell me and my sister all the time that our wants and our needs are two different things. Well who decides what our wants and needs are? SOOO.... yea! Another thing my mom use to say when we asked her for outrages stuff was, "People in hell want ice water". I know everyone says these phrases but at a young age I thought my mom was telling me to go to hell in a very nice way, mom always had us laughing at her weird phrases. Now I use them with

my kids, they all grown now so I can do that.

On July 25th, 2002, I wrote in my journal, ('The greatest book you can ever read is your own.") That stands true to this day in my life. I was going through hard times and I was really feeling down on myself. I had had two more kids and was in a relationship that really didn't exist. I was in love with the wrong man at that time and all I wanted was real love. I was going back and forth with my kids' dad and he cheated on me left and right, but I still took him back. We dated other people from time to time, but we still manage to keep getting back together. I missed out on some promising relationships because of him. I sat back and read my journals that I had from 1998 to 2009 and realized that I was completely insane with a man that didn't want me. I put him before God and my kids. I gave him my all and accepted the fact that he was seeing other women. I was really a fool in my late twenty's and early thirties. I couldn't do anything but shake my head at half of the mess that I wrote.

Jody, my Jody, I got that line from the movie Baby Boy. I hated that movie with a passion because I thought someone had read my journal and made a movie about my life with Jody. Of course, his name wasn't Jody but that's what I called him after seeing that movie. I watched it once and never again, to this day have I chose not to see it again, I can cry now just for even thinking about it. The thing is, he is a spectacular father but when it came to relationships, he SUCKED at it! On the other hand, you have to think about it, we were young, in our twenties, and how many twenty something year old's really want to be tied down in one relationship?

I always felt that in our twenties we supposed to do stupid things, in our thirties, we clean up the stupid stuff we did in our twenties. Then in our thirties, we finally recognize what little time we have left and try to make the most of it. Now I'm in my forties and this is the time to get off your butt and finally enjoy life and do what's best for me. The kids are old enough to take care of themselves once they have moved out with their own kids and you have time to sit back and begin your life. In your forties, you become smarter, stronger, and more God fearing. By the time you reach your fifties, the golden years, you should be able to tell your children that are in they twenties to straighten the hell up because life stops for no man.

As I reflect on my entire life, I have to honestly say, that I was blessed. I had to look at all the times that I could have died, I could have gotten a uncurable diseases, my children could have been out of control and I could still be stripping or at least have my own strip club.

How many women own a strip club? Not many, but it was an option at one point.

I pushed people away because I was afraid to love and go experiment with life. I let some much hold me down and keep me from walking in my gifts. Here I am in my forties and the only thing I can say right now is "Thank you God for sparing my life and my kids' life. DAMN! What was I thinking back then!?"

The older I got I started to realize that nobody can make you happy on this earth. It is up to you and your choices how your life turns out. We cannot blame God or the devil every time something bad happens because it's all in your choices. God doesn't mess with freewill; you make your choices however you chose to, and He will be with us every step of the way if you choose to believe He will. We can't blame everything on the devil all the time, God gave us freewill to pick door A or door B. Some people might even argue with me about that statement and that's fine. The devil is happy with all the bad choices we make. So, to make matters worse he adds pain and furry to our lives, we opened the door for our troubles and there he is laughing and waiting. Everyone is entitled to their own opinion, I'm not by far, giving props to the devil or trying to take up for him because I've seen him face to face before, I'm just saying that we have to take responsibility for our own choices. We will see the face of God one day and he will show us our entire life right in front of Him and there will be no way you could talk your way out of it or say the devil made me do it. Now I am a true believer that the devil can enter into people because they are weak and vulnerable. People can invite the devil in and don't even know it, also the devil can live in people you thought you loved the most.

When I was a young girl, my mother was married to a guy she thought she loved so much. After her and my dad got divorced a few years past by before she married again. This man was everything she could have wanted, and treated her like royalty, until he started to get mad at her for no reason. That's when I saw the devil for the first time in my life and his name was Charles.

I believe I was between the age of five or six when my mother was married to the devil. I used to see this man tie my mother to the pipes in the bathroom under the sink and beat her till she passed out. I used to see him come home from work and my mom would be sitting on the couch watching TV with us and he would just grab her and take her to the bedroom and beat her for no reason. I remember one time he had locked her in the bedroom for two days and my sister had to feed me out of the garbage can in the kitchen because he wouldn't' let her feed us or let my mother out. Many, many, nights we could her our mother in the room crying and screaming for someone to help her. My sister and I was young, it wasn't anything we could do to help her. It became the norm for us, we could hear him beat and rape my mother as we sat there watching bugs bunny because we had gotten so us to it by then.

But God! One day we were home, he came home and started in on my mother because he had a bad day at work, he began to beat her in front of us. I heard her scream, "Not in front of my children! please!" so he took her into the bedroom and continued and I ran outside. Well, this particular day, our neighbor came over because she heard my mother screaming from inside the house and she knocked on the door. My sister didn't open the door because she didn't want to get in trouble. Our neighbor heard all the commotion in the home, so she went and got her husband Vincent and his two friends, I think one of their names was Tom or something, they tried to get into the house to see what's going on. He came to the door and looked in the living room window, he saw my sister and I on the floor crying and he heard my mother screaming from the other room. Before we knew it, he had burst through the living room window with his wife and she grabbed us and took us out of there while her husband went into the room that my mom was in, they kicked the door down and beat the HELL! out of that demonic demon that was attacking my mother. They grabbed us and took us all away. We never seen that bastard again.

I always told God and my husband that if I ever seen that man again, I will kill him on the spot, no questions asked, no reason, no hesitation. Then I will sit and wait patiently on the cops to come take me away. I won't cause any problems, I won't reset arrest, I would just sit there with a cigarette in my mouth and a Harley Quinn smile on my face. I would gladly do my jail time with a smile on my face. At one time, I had no intentions on wanting to kill him. If I ever saw him again, I would rather torture him for at least a month so he could feel all the pain he bestowed upon my mother. This man use to have blood come out his eyes like tears, why wouldn't I want to send him packing back to hell? We would just be down in hell there together. I do not care, and I mean that from the bottom of my heart and I almost got my wish.

One day my daughter, who was 18 at the time, and my best friend went to the grocery store to pick up a few things. We all were standing on the cereal aisle and a man was standing some ways down from us and he kept staring in our direction. I thought he was slick trying to flirt with my best friend, so we didn't pay it no mind. He looked familiar to me but couldn't place my hand on it. He was an old fellow, short and black as midnight with grey lowcut hair with the evilest grin I have ever seen. He walked up to us with his basket and asked me was I Eva's daughter and I said, "Why?" I was really thinking, who are you and do you know what kind of danger you about to be in".

I thought he was one of my mother's old truck driving buddies that my mom knew back in the day. So, he told me his name was Charles and when he said that, I paused for a minute in pure disbelief. My daughter had walked away to go get cookies or something by then, my best friend instantly recognized the name and pulled me away. By the time that name registered in my head my friend Lala had to pull me away from him. I stopped and turned around and he said, "You look just like your mother." Everything in God's power kept me from causing great harm to that man right there in the grocery store. In just a few seconds, I had flash backs of my sister and I eating out of the kitchen garbage cans and watching him beat my mother to a bloody pulp came rushing back to me. I started walking towards him with all the built-up anger and pain I had in my body and spirit to get ready to murder this old man right dead in front of the fruit loops cereal.

My daughter finally came back, and Lala told her to grab me because it's time to go now. Nicole asked Lala why, and Lala told her who that man was and that your mother is about to go to jail for murder. Nicole dropped what she had in her hands and we both began to come for him. It was about to be a cleanup on aisle 6 in just 3.5 seconds.

We as a family stick together no matter the consequences, that's how I raised them and that was about to happen. Lala came and jumped in front of us and said, "NO! Let God handle him! Let's go NOW!" I looked at her and didn't even recognize who she was, and I told her, "Move out my way woman because we are about to arrange the emergency meeting with him and the devil right now!" Suddenly, Lala snatched my arm and my daughters' arm and pulled us out the store. We waited in the parking lot for that bastard to make his very last exit into civilization. Lala was yelling let's go in my ear, but Nicole and I were in a state of mind that we didn't care what she was saying, we were about to commit the ultimate crime in broad day light. We didn't care about witnesses, jail, or even if that bastard had a gun on him. Trust me, if he would have pulled a gun on us, it would have been four pointing back at him. One of us was going to die that day and it wasn't going to be us.

Apparently, he knew his fate was waiting outside for him because he never came out and we waited for about an hour for him to exit so I could watch him go to is car. Lala kept going on and on about leaving, so we finally left. I went home and told my boys and then we end up having a family meeting that I cannot discuss. Forgiving certain things is very hard to do. I don't even know if I ever told my mother about that.

I'm not going to ask for forgiveness from God because I know my heart, it would be a lie and He sees it. I do hope my mother can forgive Charles for what he did to her, if not, I totally understand, I can't forgive him either so why should she? God will deal with me on that later. I do thank Charles for showing me what to look out for, maybe Z was his grandchild in his past life or the spawn of Satan or something. Either, or, I can handle both of them if they ever cross my path again. I would simple smile and say God bless you and may God be with you. Then probably set his house on fire or put him in a cage with every deadly animal known to man, then turn around and inject him with a cure and then do it all over again. I don't know, maybe something like that anyway. They can't be found if the animals eat them.... right?

Phoenix is what they call me, " *A person or thing that has become renewed or restored after suffering calamity or apparent annihilation.*" I love that meaning so much I had to say it again. God can really do some amazing things in a person life but our choice to receive it is up to us. I'm telling some of my experiences because other women can relate to what I been through. Being in a relationship with someone one for years and you never got married is a problem. Maybe they using the excuse Jody gave me, "We not financially stable yet or It's not time." 15 years together and we still didn't get married, really? How about a woman being in love with a married man whom you have been seeing for 5 years and he constantly telling you he hates his wife and he can't wait to get a divorce.

Here is the one for the ages, a woman spending more time with her man more than she does with her own kids is a big problem too, she always leaves them with grandma or the eldest sibling. I can say that, I've done it before. We as women are showing our children how to treat others and how we want to be treated. Same goes for my own daughter, she never seen a man mistreat me, disrespect me, nor put his damn hands on me. But she knows if that was to ever happen, we would all be in jail. I am that way because of what I seen my mother go through and I BE DAMN if I see anybody do that to my only daughter. The only disrespect that she seen towards me was if someone cuts me off in traffic. I am not saying this to point figures, I had to go through it myself, I never judge anybody for what they do until I hear the whole story. Lies can spread just as fast as the wind, by the time the truth comes out, no one knows what to believe anymore because other lies attached themselves on to the one that was started. Now some innocent person goes to jail, somebody got killed and family or friendship end because of one little lie or not waiting to hear the whole story.

Phoenix sat in her seat for a while in a small daze that lasted maybe 10 seconds. Once she snapped out of it, I asked her what just happen. She smiled and said she had a flashback on a few things that happened long time ago, so I asked her would she mine to share them, maybe it will help others. She looked at me and said, "Some things God doesn't stop from happening."

Phoenix rearranged herself in her seat and took a deep breath. She pulled her hair back in to a ponytail and began to speak.

A lot of people judged me because I had kids at an early age. I had

three children by the same man by the time I was 21. I love my children and I do not regret any of them. The lifestyle that I had was a
different one, it was so weird that if I told you in the exact order it
really happened in would confuse you. It seemed that I was always
dealing with the wrong people in my life. I had a secret life, only a
few knew about, and I assumed that made me look a certain way to
some people. I was just looking for comfort in all the wrong places. I
had low self-esteem and lack of attention. I am about to tell you a
story that only four people on the face of this earth knows about.

I was in love with the most popular boy in the neighborhood and
every girl in the community wanted him, so how I ended you with
him is a mystery. I was a tomboy and always played in the dirt with
the other kids from the hood. Back then, you didn't have to worry
about anybody kidnapping kids because everyone looked out for each
other's children. They can beat your butt and take you home to your
parents, so your parents can beat your butt again and send you back
outside until the streetlights came one. I stated earlier that I had kids
at a young age, and I did. To my surprise, I didn't' t know that the relationship with my oldest kids' father was a toxic one. After I told my
story to the man I was about to marry (Steven), he informed me that
what happened to me sounded like the father of my children took
advantage of me. How was that taking advantage of me if we were a
couple and I consented to everything we did? Steven told me after
what I told him about my relationship with my kid's dad, now he sees
why my sex drive was so high and all the weird things we did together
in bed explained a lot. Steven said, No, it wasn't rape, it was a form of
domination. Steven told me that Alex (not his real name), felt like he
had dominion over me and since I was in love with him, I consented
to everything. Of course, after he said that, I decided to go look up
this word domination to get the real meaning.

(**Domination**: 1; *supremacy or preeminece over another, 2; excercise
of mastery, ruling power, or preponderant influence.*)

(**Dominate**: 1 *to exert control, direction, or influence on* 2: *to have commanding positon or controlling power over* 3: *to rise high above in a position suggestion power to dominate-*)

After reciting the definition by heart, I could tell that Phoenix had read that meaning repeatedly to herself plenty of times. Her whole demeanor changed, and she started to get a bit agitated.

I'm going to give you a quick rundown on the things Alex and I did together so you can get a clear picture why Steven would say that. I will keep it clean cut and respectful because of the type of book you are writing.

I have been engaged eight times before I got married, how I had my mindset of men, the first time the messed up, I kicked them out of my life quickly. I had a 6-month rule, after 6 months, I was done with you. I refused to have any man feel they could control me or put they hands on me or my children and if they got too close too soon, I cut them off.

During the time I was dating Alex. Steven was really my first boyfriend and the one who broke my virginity. We were stupid kids who swore we were in love. That's back when the term "Going together" meant you were a couple. We dated for a while when I was in Junior High and he moved on to high school, after that, we lost touch because why would a high schooler date a junior high kid. We all still hung out though, but it was just playing football and shooting hoops together. It was cool at the time because we all were just young and dumb out here trying to be the grown at the age of 14 to 17.

Alex was Stevens friend and we all played ball together, Alex at the time was older than all of us, he was 17. He had a lot of friends because he was in the 10th or 11th grade when all of this went down, I think. He used to come by our house a lot because he would always be looking for Steven to come play football in the field behind the apartments plus, Steven was my sisters' best friend, they all were in high school together. This day Alex came to the house looking for Steven and my sister, but they had walked to store to go get $3 worth of ham and $2 worth of cheese from the corner market for lunch. My mother was in her room because she had just worked a double shift at the hospital downtown. He came to the door and I met him there before he could knock so he wouldn't wake up my mom. I went and stood by the porch to meet him and he said he was looking for Steven to play ball. I told him they walked to the store and they should be back any moment and did he want to wait on the porch with me. He said sure and began to toss the football in the air and catching it. I got off the porch to play a little one on one with him to past the time until my sister returned with lunch and we began talking. Girls from the neighborhood were walking up and down the street flirting with Alex and speaking to him. They looked at me and always said hello because folks knew I was the only girl out there that played ball, and everyone saw me as the little roughneck tomboy from the block. Nobody paid me any mind when they saw me with boys, that's just how I was.

While we were outside waiting on them to return, Alex asked me was I still dating Steven and I told him no, we're just friends. He laughed and said under his breath, "His lost." I told him I heard him and asked what that meant, and he said, " Nothing, never mind."

I didn't think anything from it and continued to play catch with him. We play for about ten more minutes then I went into the house to get us a cup of Kool-Aid because it felt like 100 and 10 degrees outside. We sat on the porch and talked about school and basketball since he was the captain. Alex asked me was I dating anyone, I said no because my mother told me I was too young for dating and I should focus on my schooling. That's when he asked me to be his girl and don't tell anyone that we would be dating, before I could answer him, my sister walked up with Steven and the conversation ended. Steven gave me this weird look and glanced at Alex with a concern look on his face, my sister told me to get in the house because I wasn't supposed to be outside while she was gone, and mother was sleeping so I grabbed the bags from my sister and went inside with her. She told Steven and Alex that we would be outside after lunch and after we cleaned the house and that they should come back in an hour. When I got in, I looked out the window and saw Steven yelling at Alex about something then Steven walked one way and Alex walked another way.

Months passed by and nothing else ever came from Alex until Steven left to go stay with his older brother Vent in Atlanta. Alex and I got closer and we began our secret relationship. When people saw us together nobody suspected a thing because he called me his little sister and he was my brother. Soon the relationship became sexual, he told me he could show me how to be a woman and that he loved me. All the girls in the hood couldn't compare to me because I was special, and I believed him."

Phoenix suddenly paused and got up to go get a drink of tea and asked me did I want some. I said sure and stopped the recorder. She walked off outside and smoked her a cigarette to clear her head I assumed so I checked to see how much space I had left on the recorder and I got up and took a bathroom break while she was outside. I wonder to myself, what could she possibly be getting ready to tell me? All the women I interviewed always came back with the most shocking stoires. What did domination have to do with any of this?

"Sorry I took so long, I had to shake some stuff off before continuing with my story". I looked at her and said, " Phoenix, please take your time, if you don't want to go into this part of your life we don't have too. Nothing will get published that you don't want published, I assure you. We can scratch this whole segment if you want. Or we can do it off the record and you can just get some things off your chest and some closer just by talking about it. I don't want you to feel you are being forced to say anything."

She looked at me and said, " I rose from the ashes, I'm fine." Enough said, I turned the recorder back on and she began.

"Alex and I started off with regular intercourse, you know, missionary style, I guess he was breaking me in or something. When Steven broke my virginity that was, the way we did it, but we only had intercourse one time. The more we had intercourse; the stranger things got. In my head, this is what all adults do, we see it in movies and in music videos, so I thought I was a real woman. Mind you, I was still in middle school. Every time we had inter-course; it was always something different. He would say let's try this position, I saw it on a movie once, so I would say ok, no matter how uncomfortable it was. I did it because I thought we were in love and I wanted to keep him happy. I enjoyed being in a secret relationship, it felt like a secret society to me. One time he took me to his room, and he had this huge mirror that took up half of his wall in his bedroom. He went to get a chair from the kitchen to bring into the room so I could have somewhere to sit. His parents and my parents were at work and my sister was at home doing a friend hair that day as usual, and folks thought I was outside playing ball.

As I watched him put the chair in front of the mirror, he asked me to sit on his lamp, so I did. We sat there and looked at each other in the mirror and he said, " Look, don't we look great together? You look better with me than you did with Steven, I knew I had to have you." I smiled and agreed. We stared at the mirror for a few more minutes then he said look in my closet and hand me some neck ties. I want you to help me pick out a tie to wear for homecoming week. I'm captain so we have to dress up and then the homecoming dance on Friday." I got up and grabbed three neck ties to match with his suits he pulled out and placed them on the bed. We looked at both suits and matched the ties up to each of them. Alex then told me that the suit tie that he was going to wear when they crown him homecoming king Friday is going to be a special one because I picked it out for him. What little did I know that the 17-year-old guy that I was in love with was about to make those neck ties very memorable.

Alex sat back in the chair and asked me did I know how to tie a necktie and of course I said no. So, he showed me, he put the tie around my neck and started looping it to form a perfectly tied necktie. Then, he asked if we could do it since no one was home and I said not today and before I knew it, he had undressed me, so I gave in. He turned me around in front of the mirror with his necktie still on me and said, " See, I told you we look good together." He smiled at me and we began to have intercourse in front of the mirror. Then he took the other two neck ties and tied them to my hands and that's how we continued. It lasted about 10 or 15 minutes and then he finished. He untied me and went to the restroom to get a towel so we can clean up after ourselves. He ran me a quick shower to clean up and then I went home........ I was on my cycle the whole time.

I stopped the recorder and stood straight up in disbelief. "He had sex with you while you were on your cycle!?" I yelled. "Yes" she said. " Phoenix! why didn't you stop him? Why didn't you tell him you were having your period?!" She smiled and said, "He knew, but that was what he wanted to do, he said it was something new he never tried before, and he didn't have on a condom." Dear sweet Jesus Phoenix! that's disgusting! Did you tell anyone about this? Sweetie, that was disgusting!"

"Yes, I told Steven many years later and now I'm telling you, my husband knows about it as well. When he heard it, he said that man better not ever cross his path here nor in the afterlife. Your reaction now is the reason no one ever knew about that day. I am ashamed and embarrassed about the whole thing. Only five people on this earth knows about that day and now others will know, just so they can feel they are not alone. It has been many times the older I got the stranger things got between us. We dated other people, but the intercourse never stopped. We never had intercourse while I was on my period ever again, but he kept coming up with more ways to do it. In the gym, on his mother's bed, in the backyard, outside in the rain, in the corner store bathroom, in front of his old girlfriend house while they were all sleeping inside late at night. It kept happening, soon, I was addicted by the time I was 18 years old. I had three children by then and all three were his, now other girls would know what to look out for. I was his toy; his little best kept secret and I loved every bit of it, then.

It stuck with me throughout the years and I guess that's why I was engaged eight times." Phoenix cracked an evil grin after she said that that gave me chills.

I told Steven all the nasty crazy things we did while I was with Alex and he had so much rage in his body that I thought he was going to hunt down Alex and beat him. People judge others without knowing the whole story, I was looked at as the fast girl from the block and labeled a whore and a slut because I had three children by the time I graduated high school. I was the only one in my class with that record. Sure, other girls had kids, but I was the only one with three. I had to fight majority of the time because of my so-called rep. Every guy wanted a piece of me because they all thought I had three baby daddies, but, no, I only had one, Alex.

We kept it a secret because I didn't want to ruin his chances of getting into a good school and going pro, mind you, he never made it out the hood. To this day, I believe he is still there with his lifelong girlfriend that he never ever married. How do I know you may ask, because I called her my best friend for five years, my ride or die chick, my ace? She betrayed me so I gave her him for payback. You cross me and I will feed you to the wolves, they are still together to this day I believe, who knows.

Steven and I broke up again because he went into the military after that and I started dating this gang member who taught me the ropes on street survival. He showed me how to survive without a man and how to protect myself from guys who weren't about nothing. Beast, was his name and that's what I will call him, he showed me that I was more than what people say about me, I was not a whore nor a slut, I was misunderstood because I had children at a young age. He told me how to get back on my feet and how to raise my children, so they won't get pulled down in this world like he did. Beast had no father nor a mother to show him the way of life, but the streets did. He taught me how to trust no one and everyone ain't your friend, not even him. God and my mother were the only things I needed to fear, how I should take no mess from anyone, not even the police.

He showed me not to ever been seen, but make sure I was heard loud and clear. I had become the woman they never saw coming. I can't elaborate on that any further because of street code. He showed me how to hustle, the art of persuasion and manipulation, and to be a Queen. To this day, I use every bit of advice he gave me only if I need it. He was very dear to me, Beast got locked up many, many, years ago and I haven't spoken to him since. Word on the streets is that he gets out soon and I can't wait to see him. He knows I'm married, and I am nothing like I use to be, He sent word to me one time that he was proud of me and that I was still his "Flaming Butterfly".

At first, I thought I was bond to be with guys who were out for one thing, control. I thought that I would never be happy because of how I lived my life in the past. I have low self-esteem, my attitude is shot to all hell, and I would snap off at the drop of a dime. I don't take no bull from anybody, that's how I lived, that is my mindset

I have been programmed to not care about you and no one else's feelings. If you weren't family, you got no love from me at all. Pure fire was my moto, I will see you burn before my I will. I stopped dating and got my life together. I graduated from college, my children are now grown and healthy, my mother and sister are well and happy and that's all I needed. Then he came into my life, and his name was Wayne.

I have a bar level that is so high when it comes to life, only God Himself can bring it down, and it crumbled when God sent me him. My dear sweet loving husband, yes, he probably married a psycho, but I have God's stamp of approval on my forehead that says, " For Wayne Only, anyone tamper with this package you will be held punishable by God's law." signed, God.

God Incorporated,

333 Heaven Gates Lane.

Kingdom of God, JC 33333

How I met him was nothing but a miracle, I had been running through men ever since I broke up with the father of my two last children. Yes, I was in deep love with him and I felt that there was no other being on this earth that can replace the love I had for him and him for me. But God had other plans. When I met Wayne, it was by pure coincidence, who knew by trying to better myself, I would see someone that would better me emotionally.

He stood there in the middle of the library glancing at the books trying to see which one he needed to check out. As he stood there, I was standing there lusting after his body. I was in college to get a better grip on life, I had just broken up with a man I was with for 15 years, why in the hell would I get myself back into the dating game again? But it was something about him that I couldn't turn my eyes away. Besides the finest butt I have ever seen on a man! He was built like a warrior, his chest like a man of steel, and a face that would make any woman stop in her tracks.

As he stood there looking through the books, a friend of his walked by and said, What's up bro?! He looked up from the books and said, "What's up mane, how you are doing?" with a huge smile on his face. His voice was soothing, hypnotizing, deep and powerful. Dear Lord!

I caught myself staring at him so long that I forgot I was supposed to be in class. My friend Lynn walked past me and saw what I was looking at. She glanced in the library and said, "Oh wow! Nice!" then she pulled my arm and said, "Not today ma'am, we have exams to take. Let's go."

When I saw him that one time, I knew that I had to have him. So, as time went on, I pursued him in my own little way. I am pleased to say, it didn't work. Everything I did to try and gain this man's attention, didn't work. Now I had to step up my game. I had never been turned down before and I was not about to be defeated. To me, he had become my ultimate goal. After many weeks of trying to get him to notice me, I finally won him over. I was able to ask him out on a date, I started asking him questions about schoolwork and study groups, then I finally asked him out on a date. He told me no, he said he was not at a point in his life right now to start seeing other people. By then, I had thrown my hands up and said forget it, I tried. By the third time, he finally said yes.

Wayne drew me closer to God, he told me things about the bible that I never even knew about. Like I said before, I knew of God, but I didn't know God. I remember one night we had dinner at his house at his house and I brought over a bottle of Mogen David. I brought wine because I knew he didn't drink, and I wanted to be respectful. Over dinner, we talked about his pass and I talked about mine. I'm surprised he didn't run for the hills when I told him what I been through. Anyway, I asked him questions about the bible that I always wanted to know. Like, how do you know the bible is true, how do you know when God is around, and was Jesus really coming back? After I asked so many questions, he said he felt like he was being tested by God to see how much he knew. But it was just me being curious because I was dating a man of God. I never dated a holy man before and things were always different. The things I was used to doing, I didn't do any more, he changed me in so many ways, but it was for the good. I gave up so many bad habits that if I were to do any of those habits today, I would probably throw up.

One day I was sitting at home and I asked God what he was doing in my life. Why did he bring Wayne into my life, or shall I say, why did I have that strong urge to be with this man? I asked God was Wayne the man I was supposed to be with? Sometimes we have to watch what we ask God because we might not be ready for His answers.

That night I asked God was Wayne special and was he the one for me, I had just had girl's night with a few of my friends and we hung around the house playing games and just socializing, catching up on old times. Around 1a.m. everyone left, I took a shower and got ready for bed. I peeped in on my kids to make sure they were ok then I went to my room.

That night, I had the strangest dream. In my dream, I was running through this dark alley way. I couldn't hardly see what I was running from, but I knew whatever I was running from was trying to kill me. As I ran through this alley, I turned around and saw some demon like creatures running towards me and they were jumping off the buildings, climbing walls, and clawing at the air. The faster I ran, the faster they ran. Soon I turned down another alley, but this alley had a small piece of light showing in a wall. Soon as I saw some light, I decided to run towards it. I hid behind some crates that was leaned up against the wall so the creatures wouldn't see me. I sat there for a minute contemplating on if I should make a break for it. The light in the crack of the wall got brighter, so, I decided to lean over to see where the light was coming from because maybe someone can help me. After I saw these creatures run pass me, I jumped up and ran towards the light. The closer to the light I got, the bigger the crack became. By then, the crack in the wall was big enough for ne to go through it, so I took my chances and ran into the light.

Right then, the creatures had found me, and I saw them charging towards me. Right when one of the creatures grabbed my leg, I was already in the light. I fell inside the crack and the cracked closed completely. What I seen when I got up was unexplainable. I stood up and realized that I was standing in a field of gold, or what looked like gold. As I gathered myself together, I looked around and realized that I was standing in a golden wheat field. It was the most beautiful thing I had ever seen. The field literally lit up like gold. When I turned to see exactly where I was, I noticed two people walking towards me. One man hand on a pair of black dress pants with a white button done shirt on and the other man was wearing a white robe of some sort, but I could not see his face. The closer they got, neither of the men saw me or noticed that I was standing there. When they got closer, I realized that the man with the white button-down shirt was Wayne. He was walking side by side with the man in the white robe. I saw Wayne smiling from ear to ear and he never took his eyes off the person he was walking with. They were engaged in a deep conversation, I guess. The closer they got; I still could not see the man he was walking with face. Wayne reached out his hand to me, I grabbed it and we all walked through the field together. Wayne never took his eyes from the man in the white robe and I never saw his face. I felt comfort and peace for a split second, then I woke up. When I woke up, I hurried to grab a piece of paper to write down my dream so I could tell it to Wayne.

He told me after reading it that he was walking with Jesus and that it was my demons chasing me in my dream down the dark alley. He told me that his walk with God was the most important thing in his life right now and that the dream was telling me that I will be walking with them together, for the rest of my life. When Wayne told me that, I knew then that God had sent Wayne to me. God had chosen a man that is totally opposite of what I was use too. I wasn't looking for Wayne and he wasn't looking for me. God arranged it for us to meet, for him to turn me down when I practically threw myself at him and for our union to be blessed by God. I asked God for a sign and he gave me one that night in a dream that I would never forget.

That was eleven years ago, and we have been happily married ever since.

My story is a story of foolishness, stupidity, strength and courage. All in all, God was with me the whole time. No matter what I been through in life, I still came out of it as a phoenix rising from my ashes stronger than ever. Life is like playing dodge ball, once you're in the game, you want to make sure that you're still standing when the game is over. Here I am, standing in my ashes, ready to take on the world with the protection of His word, the Armour of God, and the strength of ten thousand men. All I want to do is here Him say in the end is, "Well done, my good and faithful servant, well done."

My life was a crazy one, through the good and the bad, God always brought through. My name is Phoenix Rising, and I am, The Daughter of God."

CHAPTER 9
FAITH AND THE TREES

"He is like a tree planted by water, that sends out its roots by the stream, and does not fear when heat comes, for its leaves remain green, and is not anxious in the year of drought, for it does not cease to bear fruit." Jeremiah 17:8

Ever since I was a little girl, I had a passion for trees. My grandparents always wanted trees in their backyard because my grandfather loved the shade that the trees provided, and my grandmother loved the fruit that they bare. Down in the south part of Tylertown Mississippi, not too many trees grew fruit back in those parts. When I was younger, my grandmother use to tell me different stories about different trees. Some trees were magical, some were healers, and some even spoke to her. She told me that trees were one of Gods favorite things, why, because the roots go deep into the earth. Grandma Rose was one of the wises and smartest women I knew, she always had things to say about plants, trees, and the Lords love. No matter what situation we came to her with, she always connected it to the trees.

My name is Faith, I am 92 years young, and this is my message for you.

As a young girl, my outlook on life was different from other kids. I always thought in the back of my head that I was born to do something special in my life. Back then, black folk had to fight to survive every day, I was born a year before the great depression happened. I remember years after the depression and I was a little older, I overheard my father and his friends one day while sitting on the back porch sipping tea, "Man, I never knew it was a great depression, we been depressed for a long time, we use to it. We the first ones to get laid off and the last ones to get hired for a job." Then, I heard my father say, "Praise the Lord anyway, nothing lasts forever." That's when I heard my momma say, "As long as we have good strong trees, we will be ok."

Grandma Rose had a fascination with one particular type of peach tree, the name of the peaches were called 'reliance peach'. She cared for that peach tree more than anything in the world. She used to say, "Baby girl, the word reliance means, dependence on or trust in someone or something. The way we depend on the good Lord to guide us, protect us, to feed us when we are hungry, and to shelter us from the storms in life. The reliance peach is a peach that is cold and hard, they need special attention in order for them to grow. The pink flowers that grow on the trees make the yard look magnificent in the spring. I got this tree working from the Henderson's that came from up north. The wife, Mrs. Anna, loved her home in North Carolina but her husband got a fancy job down here in good ole Tylertown, Mississippi and they had to move.

BEFORE HENDERSON'S MOVED, HER MAID, BERTHA MAY, GAVE her a small tree that was shoved inside of a glass flowerpot. Bertha told her, "Mrs. Anna, if you take good care of this here peach tree, it will grow strong and beautiful with the best peaches you ever had.

Those peaches will feed you and other families to come. Care for it, nurture it, love on it like you love God, and never, ever let it die."

Mrs. Anna did exactly what she said. That peach tree grew tall and wide, the widest any one had ever seen. The more it grew, Mrs. Anna decided to take the seeds and plant then in the grown to produce more trees. After a while, Mrs. Anna had a field full of peach trees, and it did exactly what Bertha May said it would do, Mrs. Anna had enough reliance peach trees to give to family, friends, neighbors, and still had enough to share with travelers. Mrs. Kris? Go look out the kitchen window for me and tell me what you see."

"Yes, ma'am." I said. I got up to proceed to go to her kitchen window. I pulled the curtains back to see a field of pink flower petals scrolled along the ground, the tress had the most perfect peaches hanging on them that lit up the yard. It was so beautiful; I had never seen anything like this before in my life. The window was cracked a bit and the smell of flowers with a sweet peachy fragrance filled the air. Birds were chirping, butterflies were flying, and the wind had a cool breeze to it. The sun beamed on those trees like God shines through the clouds. It was the most beautiful experience I had ever encountered. I gazed at the rows of trees for a minute longer then I walked back to the dining room table.

"Mrs. Faith, that was a beautiful yard back there, how did you do it?" Mrs. Faith put her cup of tea down, smiled, and said, "Well, it was all love. You see, when you get a seed, you must take care of it, feed it, grow it, and talk to it. The trees hear everything, and they respond from it. If you show any plant love, that plant will show it back."

I looked at her and said, "I truly believe that, my mom and my grandmother always talked to their plants. The one's inside the house and outside. I always thought that they were just talking to themselves because they were bored or had something on their minds. My mom named all of her plants, they grew so big that she had to break them down and repot them in other flowerpots so it could grow more. Interesting."

I reached down to grab the tea she offered me, "Mrs. Faith? What kind of tea is this? It's amazing. Don't tell me, it's peach tea, and the peaches are from your trees." She looked at me laughing and said, "No, it's Lipton iced tea from the can, I mixed the powder with water and sugar like everyone else." Then we both started laughing.

She put her cup down and wiped her mouth with a handkerchief. "Darling" she said, let me tell you why you are here. I have a friend who has a friend with a daughter named, Grace, who has a friend named Tracey. They told me all about what you are doing and why you are writing this book. Once I heard about you, I told them that I wanted to meet you and tell you in person how happy I am that someone is doing something like this that's close to home. All my life, I never had anybody to ask me, what my view of life is, or how I made it to 92 years of age with no health problems, no money problems, no mental issues or anything. When people see me, they just assume I have diabetes, high blood pressure, on arthritis meds, and all kinds of stuff. Well, I asked them to contact you because I would like to know if I can be in your book? I'm pretty sure that I would be the oldest one, so, I decided to ask. And here you are, sitting on my leather couch sipping Lipton tea with me. So, what do you think?"

I was sitting there shocked an amazed that a woman, that lived 5 hours and 316 miles from me heard about what I was doing and wanted to meet me. I knew then that this was all God's doing, Praise be His name!.

"Mrs. Faith, it would be an honor to have you be a part of the Daughters of God, you would really be the final peace to this amazing journey. I will need you to sign some papers authorizing me to keep you identify safe and to make sure only the parts you want in here would be written. Is that ok?"

For a minute she didn't say anything which concerned me for a minute. I was wondering did I offend her or maybe she didn't understand what I was saying. Then, she spoke, "Precious, I don't need to sign anything, I am 92 years old and I asked you to take down my story, not you are asking me, big difference. I'm too old in the game already to be doing paperwork and watching what I say about my life. Baby, just take notes, write down what I say, and we can begin."

At that moment, I couldn't concentrate on anything, I was too busy being shocked that this lady just said she was too old in the game already. How did no one else here this? I was literally trying my hardest to keep from laughing. Instantly, I knew this lovely young lady was about to blow my mind. I'm sorry, I couldn't hold it anymore, I burst out into laughter so hard, I couldn't catch my breath and tears were rolling down my face. After I got it halfway out of my system, she looked over at my and said,

"You caught that didn't you? when I said I was too old in the game? That's good you laughed out loud, that tells me a lot about you. To me, that tells me that you are an honest woman. That tells me that you actually listened to every word I said and that you were paying attention to detail. Nice. Not many people would have laughed out like that. Do you know why? Well because in this world, people hide their true emotions. They let people say and do all kinds of things to them. Some people see things and walk right past it because it doesn't concern them, or people are so worried about what others think about them, so they hide behind the mask that they take off at home, at night, when no one is looking. I said that same thing to a young lady last week at the dollar store my son Jason drove me too and the young lady looked at me, smiled and said nothing else. Once I got to the register, I looked over at the other checkout line and there that young lady was with two of her friends looking at me and Jason standing in line. This time she was whispering and pointing her finger at us and snickering with her head turned so I wouldn't see her laugh. Now Mrs. Kristina, what does that tell you?"

'Well", I said, "That tells me that those females are full of ..... , I'm sorry, that tells me that you should have sent Jason over there to ask them were they ok and who were they laughing and pointing their fingers at."

"No need for that precious, she said, 'I knew what they were laughing at because I gave them the reason to do it. I wasn't mad, I was educated." I glanced at her with a confused look on my face and said, "You got educated, but, how?" She put her tea down and reached over to grab a piece of paper, she wrote something on it and balled it up in her hands. Then she said, "Can you take this to the trash for me?' I said, "Sure". I walked to the kitchen and threw the paper in the trash and came back to sit down.

"Do you know why I wasn't upset with those girls, because that's how they are all the time, they're like that with each other. They hold in things like secrets, lies, thoughts, feelings, and emotions. People are so afraid to live their best life that they cover it up because they have to get peoples approval. Why? When I told her the same thing I said to you, she would rather smile in my face, hold in the laughter until she was around her friends to sneak and talk about it on the low. That's how fights and rumors get started. Folks would rather hide their true selves than to let a laugh go, or a smile, or even a helping hand. Since when do we have to seek approvable for how we want to feel, or I'm only going to laugh if my friends laugh first."

"Mrs. Faith, what if the young lady was showing you respect, and she didn't want to laugh in your face? Now I feel that I disrespected you for laughing. Also, what if they thought your mind was slipping and she was just showing you respect? How could you determine any of that? Does that mean people talking behind others back out of respect?"

"No, she said, that means she didn't pay attention to what I said in the moment. Then when it dawned on her what I said, she ran told her friends then they started laughing and pointing fingers at us.

Think about it, if she would have heard what I said loud and clear then she would have laughed and said something nice back. Instead, it took a minute for her to realize what I said then she hid herself to go laugh about it. People never live in the moment anymore. If it's funny laugh and comment on it. There is nothing wrong with that, if she would have stopped for a second and said something back, then she would have known that I was in my right mind and she would have avoided all the other stuff she did.

The reason trees are so special in our family is because God helps it grow. Trees grow straight up; they last for years to come and they are deeply rooted to the earth. Yes, we do our part in planting it, but God does the rest. We all have to be like trees when it comes to God and His love. We need to raise up our branches and let Him do the rest. When the trees are thirsty, God knows because it rains. When the trees feel hungry, they go deeper into the earth and God provides them with food, and when they trees need strength to withstand the storms, he makes their foundation stronger. It's the same with us, we raise our hands to the Lord when we need Him, He feeds us if we are hungry, He strengthens our foundation when we feel we are about to fall. So if God can put as much love into a tree, what makes us think that he won't do the same for us.

I am a healthy 92-year-old woman because I lived my life with the instructions. We come into this world with instructions not destruction. Everything we need to know is in His word. Will we have things that will be roadblocks for us? yes, we will. Will we have pain and hurt, yes, we will, will we have times when we want to scream out to God and say, "What are you doing up there!" Most definitely, but that doesn't men we have to stop loving Him, trusting Him, and falling to His feet for forgiveness or for strength.

I don't' have to tell you my life story, I don't have to tell you the good or bad that I went through in my life, as you can see, I'm still here. I believe God put us all here to fulfill a purpose, we don't know what that purpose is until we've done it. Why does God still have me here for 92 years, I don't know, but whatever it is, I haven't fulfilled my mission yet because I'm alive and kicking. Life is so beautiful if people would just open their hearts to seeing the real world. Look beyond the crimes, beyond the deaths and violence that's going on. Look to the sky, God never changes, the sky is always blue, the trees are always green, and the love is always the same.

If you have a dream and a passion to do something, then do it. Don't wait until your old and too tired to try. Do it as soon as God put it in your heart. Every person I seen in my lifetime that has followed their dreams with God in the mist of it, have been happy. The ones who followed their dreams and it failed, means they didn't have God with them, or they were doing it for worldly reason's and not positive reasons. You feel it in your heart, you feel it in your soul, you wake up thinking about it, you go to bed thinking about it, then honey, that's what you supposed to be doing.

I wanted to be in your story because it's my duty to tell others out there that if you trust God to the fullest, give Him your all, help your brother and sisters when you can, forgive, be honest, and talk to God every day, I promise you that you will feel the love of God all through your life. Ask Him and He will give it to you, talk to Him and He will talk back to you, search for Him and He will find you.

Those trees outside gave me life, and God gave them life. When I get to a point where I need a little help, I look to the trees. I go out to care for them, talk to them, and nurture them because God will be in the mist of the trees. When I wan to talk to God, I go to the yard and walk amongst the trees. I'll hear a slight whisper, or I'll see a sign that indicates that God is listening. We have learned to trust God no matter what, I am saying this with deep sincerity in my heart, trust Him through everything and He will be there when you call Him.

I have lived in this town a very long time. All of my friends are gone home to be with the Lord. My only family now is my son Jason and his three wonderful sons. When I finally leave this place, I know that my trees will be taken care of and that I would have served my purpose on earth. Did you know that the peach tree that Bertha May gave Mrs. Harrison is still standing in the backyard? I don't remember if I told you that or not. Like I told you, the roots run deep, and they run strong. Take that with you when you go, keep the roots grounded, loved, and cared for, and everything else will grow into a wonderful tree with branches that spread their arms out to the sun(Son).

My name is Faith and that's all you need to know.

(To my readers: I want to inform you that Mrs. Faith passed away three days after my visit with her. Her son Jason told me that he found her outside, sitting under the oldest peach tree she had in her field. She was holding the bible in one hand and a balled-up piece of paper in the other hand that read, "I'm ready Lord" written inside.)

Her purpose was completed, may God cradle her in His arms and receive her into His Kingdom. Amen

AFTERWORD

In the end, I had the pleasure of meeting with these extraordinary women. I cried with them, laughed with them, and felt the same pain with them. I've learned that no matter how the outside picture may look, it's always a story behind that pretty smile, that glowing personality, and that beautiful face. Deep down, everyone carries scars of their past. No matter where you're from, what country you leave in, and how good or bad your life could be, everyone has a story that we all can learn from.

When I finished with all my interviews and formed them together into this book, I couldn't help but notice that these women were all connected in some way. Some of the women stayed out of town in other cities, and some were local. Yet, they all were linked some kind of way. I heard my Pastor say many times, "We are all the same in God's eyes." I would have to say, I agree. From the testimony of **Heaven Gates**, to the confession of the twins, **Grace and Mercy**, we all have accomplished something in our lives that God was right there to see them through. Even when we felt that His presence wasn't there, He was there with us the whole time.

Being with those women gave me the strength I needed to pursue my writing dream full time. Fear is no longer a factor in my life, the fear of failure, the fear of rejection, and the fear of not being accepted is no longer an issue for me. When I begin to think of fear, I will remember the strength of **Eva**, when I feel that my life is falling apart, I will think of **Lilly**. When I want to feel connected with God, I will look to the tress like **Faith**. When I feel lost, I will pray for knowledge and search for God, just like **Wisdom** did. I will think about **Treasure** if something doesn't sit right in my spirit, and I will fight like **Storm** and rise from the ashes like a **Phoenix**.

Each of these women had a gift and they used their gifts God gave them to become powerful women that we've grown to love and be proud of in many ways.

But as for me, all of these ladies became a part of my life, and I will carry their stories with me forever. These passionate women, these sisters of mine in Christ Jesus, created and have become, "The Daughters of God"

ABOUT THE AUTHOR

Mrs. Kristina S. Franklin was born in Shreveport Louisiana at Barksdale Air Force Base in 1977. Her parents, Karen Jackson Smith and Chester D. Ward had two children, Mrs. Franklin and her eldest sister Mrs. Nina Taylor. Mrs. Franklin is the wife of Jeffrey D. Franklin, Sr. of nine years, they both have a blended family of eight and three wonderful granddaughters.

She holds two college degrees, AA in Health Information Management from National College of Business and Technology and a BS Degree in Human Services from Lancaster Bible College.

Mrs. Franklin grew up in Orange Mound in Memphis, TN during most of her childhood. Her mother showed her and her sister how to survive and make ends meet with very little, along with teaching them the value of family sticking together. Her grandmother, Mrs. Annie Jackson taught her how to be a lady at all times, her grandfather taught her how to follow the rules of life, and the streets taught her how to survive and protect yourself at all cost.

Kristina always had a gift for writing, she has been writing short stories since she was eight years old for fun. Her mother always called her an animated little child because she could make a story and act it out with any word they give her. In 2001 she wrote her first unpublished book entitled "Maya's Storm" and now she is the author of her first book, "The Daughters of God". She started letting people see her talent when she joined her home church, "Christ In You Faith

Temple" when she married her husband and became a member. Ever since then, she is the writer of all plays and skits that the church holds thanks to her Senior Pastor, Pastor Tommie L. Brown Jr.

Now she has begun to create her own company called "Kingdom Builders Outreach Services" where she mentors young adults and adults with everyday life issues and helps them see the things in life that they don't see. Her contributions and her book and other books to come, are to let others see that life can be better if you know that someone else has overcome bad situations.